Jerusalem, Jerusalem

Jerusalem,

Jerusalem

by Lesley Hazleton

The Atlantic Monthly Press
BOSTON / NEW YORK

FIRST EDITION

Chapter 12 appeared in *Moment Magazine.*

LIBRARY OF CONGRESS CATALOGING-IN-PUBLICATION DATA

Hazleton, Lesley.
Jerusalem.

1. Hazleton, Lesley.   2. Jerusalem — Biography.
3. Israel — Politics and government.   4. West Bank —
Politics and government.   5. Jewish-Arab relations.
I. Title.
DS109.86.H395A34   1986   956.94'4   86-1223
ISBN 0-87113-064-5

"The Second Coming" from THE POEMS by W. B. Yeats, edited
by Richard J. Finneran, reprinted with permission of Macmillan Publishing Company. Copyright 1924 by Macmillan Publishing Company, renewed 1952 by Bertha Georgie Yeats.

Passage from ISRAEL'S LEBANON WAR by Ze'ev Schiff and Ehud
Ya'ari reprinted with permission of Simon & Schuster, Inc. Copyright
1984 by Ze'ev Schiff and Ehud Ya'ari, translation © 1984 by Ina
Friedman.

Abridged selection "I Came Back Once More" from GREAT
TRANQUILITY: QUESTIONS AND ANSWERS by Yehuda Ami-
chai reprinted with permission of Harper & Row Publishers, Inc.
Copyright 1983 by Yehuda Amichai. Translated from the Hebrew by
Glenda Abramson and Tudor Parfitt.

RRD

Published simultaneously in Canada

PRINTED IN THE UNITED STATES OF AMERICA

*For Dot and Pantz and Yshai and Noa and Yoni,
lifelong friends, with love and breakfast*

Author's Note

MANY of the people in this book are my friends, and we talked with all the love, doubt, anxiety and hope that friends express to each other. Since some of them are very public figures, and others very private, I have sometimes used only first names, altering those names to protect their confidence. My thanks to all these people for their trust and support, and thanks too to my editor, Joyce Johnson, and my agent, Gloria Loomis.

Jerusalem, Jerusalem

I

IT was *hamsin* when I arrived. The dry wind had come in off the desert weeks before, creating a haze of heat and dust. A whole landscape waited for the first rain to break the spell of sultriness. The rain was late, and people were getting almost mystical about it, as though it meant something. They were waiting, tense as the air itself, for the spell to break.

Exhausted from the long plane trip, I slept. But it was a restless *hamsin* sleep, full of strange dreams, and I came wide awake in the middle of the night, dry and dusty and thirsty.

I took some water and went out onto the terrace. The hazy silver of the full moon cast enough light to see. That, and the lightning playing behind Mount Zion, flashing on down over the desert hills to the Dead Sea. There was no thunder, just this air electric with tension. It was a night very like the one twenty years before, when I had stood on this same terrace and decided to stay.

Mount Zion still rose gently into the dark, a soft silhouette with stone walls winding round it. At the top was the pointed dome of the Dormition Abbey. Mary died here, and as they tell small children, *dormit* — she fell asleep. Beside it, the tower of David's Tomb looked like a minaret. I narrowed my eyes and managed to re-create the illusion discovered by each generation of Jerusalem children: viewed at the right angle, the clockface at the top of the tower takes on the profile of a Prussian soldier, helmet, mustache and all.

To one side, the battlement walls of the Old City stretched along the hill, too familiar to be forbidding. To the other, the black space of the valley curved down into the distance like a huge yawn of night and stone, mysterious and beckoning.

The valley was Gei ben Hinnom. In English, that name contracts into Gehinnom, and then into Gehenna. The biblical hell. The valley of death. Thousands of years ago, Moloch stood here: a great iron statue with fires burning year-round in its belly. Infants were sacrificed to Moloch. They were thrown alive into that fire in its belly. Thrown in atonement, perhaps, or in appeasement. In hope or in despair. Moslem legend has it that if you stand here on a quiet night, you can hear the souls of the dead crying out. But I never heard them, not even when Gehenna was no-man's-land. And all I heard now, as I stood on the edge, was one lone dog crying forlornly into the still air of the night.

The thick stone walls of the building behind me glowed pale in the moonlight. It was old Jerusalem stone, hewn rough and large by masons who built, not for themselves, but for centuries. There is a quality to old stone that makes short shrift of human time. It lifts you out of the wary human rhythm of hours and days into another dimension where time telescopes and expands, freeing the mind to roam over the framework of years with no sense of distance. So much time had passed since I first stood on this spot, yet it felt as though I were still twenty, and still amazed to find myself here.

Thunder sounded far off, reverberating through the hills. But the sound didn't pass. Instead, it grew louder, more insistent, a heavy rolling lumbering sound coming closer and closer. Finally it took shape. A line of tank carriers moved slowly down the road by the Old City wall. They changed gear beneath Mount Zion, and the engines strained as they bore their loads up out of the valley. The tank cannons pointed eerily ahead into the night, their muzzles, muffled by tarpaulin wraps, looking like small fists at the end of long thin arms. I remembered that this was the route used by the armored corps to move from one desert training ground to another.

More dogs barked as the tanks rumbled off into the distance. I had come back to the present. So much had happened and so much changed since I had first come here. I reminded myself that it was another time — even another place, another country.

"What am I doing here?" I asked myself. "I thought I'd left."

✡

It was the second tough question that had been asked that day. On the plane, the American couple sitting beside me inquired innocently where I was from. It is a simple question for most people, its answer the starting point of identity. But for me it had become a minefield. London, Jerusalem, New York . . . I had too many answers, and none of them sufficient. Even my bylines reflected the confusion. I could be an Israeli journalist, or a British psychologist, or a British-Israeli journalist and psychologist working in New York. It depended on the subject or the whim of the editor. Dual nationality is a tricky business when it comes to identity. I had mumbled an answer on the plane and then turned the question back on them, admiring the confidence of their reply.

My answer too had once been clear: Jerusalem.

I went to Israel for two weeks in 1966, discovered Jerusalem, and stayed for thirteen years. I stayed at first because I was twenty and in love. After the dark damp of England with its chilly couplings under layers of blankets, Ariel and I were blithe spirits, naked on the bed, on the flagstone floor, even on the rooftop. I called my university that I would not be coming back to do my doctorate. And a short time after, when romance had waned and I knew enough Hebrew to realize that Ariel, despite his name, was neither blithe nor spiritual, it was too late to change my mind. The halls of English academe do not forgive impetuosity.

But I was bolstered by that youthful grace of a passionate commitment to whatever I said or did. I had no regrets. Doubt played no part in my life then. Ariel had fulfilled his role and stepped gracefully off stage. I never heard from him again, and never minded. I was already developing the fierce pride of being a Jerusalemite.

It had to be fierce. The city was still divided then, by the long swathe of barbed wire and fire walls that marked off no-man's-land. An occasional blast cut into the night as some creature leaped on a mine or as a small boy from one side or the other, dared into forbidden territory, ended his game in tragedy.

Down in the comfort of the coastal plain, the worldly denizens of Tel Aviv had little time for Jerusalem. It was a city of academics and mystics, they said. A small provincial city perched on a mountain ridge between desert to the east and pine forests to the west. I loved it as an underdog of cities, its beauty in its shabby forlorn quiet, its crumbling stone.

Nobody told me there would be a war. If they had, I doubt if it would have made any difference. The idea of war wasn't real for me then. I was innocent.

For me, as for Israel, the following years brought a loss of innocence. I learned more than I ever wanted to know about war. And more than I ever hoped to know about peace. Until in 1979, exhausted from too much tension, too much excitement, too much passion, I left. I moved to New York. And in the years since, I had tried in vain to come to terms with that leaving.

Each year I came back to visit, and each time, I reentered the confusion between "here" and "there." It ran through my letters, my conversations, my mind. I no longer knew which place was which. Sitting in New York, I would speak like a Jerusalemite, saying "here" when I meant Jerusalem. In Jerusalem, a New Yorker in me would suddenly appear and refer to Jerusalem as "there." It wasn't just jet lag. The mind lags far behind the jet. I no longer knew quite where I was, or where I belonged.

In New York I would talk about Israelis as "they" — and then lapse into the Israeli way of thinking, saying "we." Each morning, I would scan the *New York Times* for news from Israel, and only then read the rest of the paper. Every year, I'd renew my subscriptions to the overseas editions of Israeli papers for one year only, thinking that in a year's time I wouldn't need them anymore, I'd have made the break. But every year I realized that I still hadn't made it. And though I generally tried to avoid other Israelis in New York, I still found a solace in their company — the company of people torn the same way, living one life in their minds and another in their hearts.

I lived this way for five years, and then in the fall of 1984 decided to make the break once and for all. I would go on a final trip back and consciously work at making my farewell to this place that pulled so insistently at mind and heart.

Ten weeks to do what five years had not achieved . . .

I couldn't go back to my own house in Yemin Moshe, the tiny village below the windmill on the slope of Gehenna, facing Mount Zion. I had sold it in the meantime. That too was part of my attempt to leave. I came back instead to Mishkenot Sha'ananim, the long row of former almshouses that were the first buildings of Yemin Moshe, and whose name translates as "tranquil dwellings." In the seventies, they had been converted into a guesthouse of the Jerusalem Municipality, set aside for visiting intellectuals, artists and scholars. By staying there, I would ensure that I was merely a visitor. But I requested the room at the end — the room where I had stayed in 1966, when I first came to Jerusalem.

Then it had been a slum. A young Yemenite woman named Tova lived there, with her blind grandmother. They cooked on a small kerosene stove. There was no hot water. The toilet was a hole in the ground carved into the stone of the hillside at the back of the house, with cement footrests on either side of it. I was young and lost, fresh off the plane from London, and they were kind to me, offering me a bed until I found my feet.

Each morning that summer, I woke to the dawn sound of church bells ringing and muezzins calling as the faithful of another country, just a hundred yards away, rose to prayer. I was in Israel; those sounds came from Jordan. Between us lay Gehenna — barbed wire and mines and thorns and ruins. I was a romantic twenty-year-old living on the edge of no-man's-land, and after the sturdy certainties of England, life on the edge was irresistible.

I sat out on the long terrace that fronted Mishkenot and watched for hours as sheep and goats roamed the steep slope below the Old City walls, dots of black and white and brown nuzzling among the stones for thorns. Sometimes the Bedouin shepherds called a greeting. The sound echoed across the dangerous still space, and my own echo wafted back to them. By late afternoon, the lowering sun would begin to cast the whole scene in Old Master colors, clearing away the bright blinding haze of midday and covering everything with a rich golden patina of depth. It seemed a special grace bestowed on the city for an hour or so each day, before darkness fell. Far far away, down through the desert and across the Jordan River, the Mountains of Moab showed clear in the pastel colors of distance, orange and pink and purple, as though someone had placed a narrow frieze of wallpaper over the horizon to mark the separation of heaven and earth.

It was hauntingly beautiful, but only those with no choice lived at Mishkenot. Academics and mystics shunned it, because despite the meaning of its name, tranquillity remained elusive. Jordanian Legionnaires patrolled the battlement walls of the Old City, and they were unpredictable. Some days, they would wave. Most days they would do nothing. But there were also the odd days when, either bored or nervous, they fired. It was safer to live elsewhere.

Instead of living elsewhere, I moved into my own house in Yemin Moshe, along the hillside from Mishkenot. The whole village was a crumbling shadow of what it had been a hundred years before, when British philanthropist Moses Montefiore built it as the first settlement outside the safety of the Old City. The windmill at the top of the hill, once Montefiore's pride and joy, seemed to have shrunk into insignificance. Its flails hung tattered and awry, as though it had simply given up. Weeds and thorns had pushed up through the paving stones of the village's stepped streets, cracking them apart and keeping the local cobbler in bread and butter by providing broken sandal straps for him to mend. The houses, built of large thick stones held together with mud, had proved the ideal habitat for furry black centipedes, some four inches long. These moved with mesmerizing purposefulness over the inner walls, making them their own. Once a year, a jolly red-faced man came to spray the drains, and took time out over a glass of mint tea to tell the tale — in the greatest detail and with the greatest delight — of the largest rat he had ever caught. To be the rat catcher of Jerusalem seemed to me a very romantic occupation. I am not even sure if the post exists any longer.

Yemin Moshe, in short, was *mesquin* — that haunting Arabic word combining bathos with a very old, sad beauty, redolent of faded memories of what once had been.

Then came 1967. The Six Days War. And victory.

Jerusalem was reunited, and everything changed. Yemin Moshe, Jerusalem, Israel, I too — all changed, and yes, changed utterly.

Yemin Moshe was suddenly one of the most valued pieces of real estate in the world, right at the heart of the united city. A special development company was set up, and most of those who had lived there throughout the dangerous years were moved out. Tova and her grandmother went to Tiberias, and we lost contact. "Gentry" began to move in, renovating the crumbling houses. The village was fast becoming the most desirable neighborhood in the city.

The stony slopes of Mount Zion were gentled under planted rosemary and honeysuckle. Swirls of water sprayed lazily over them, evaporating sinfully in the dry desert air. Soon the wild forlorn beauty of abandon was gone. The formal public beauty of the landscape gardener replaced the private poignant one of neglect.

The mines and barbed wire and rubble of nineteen years were cleared out of Gehenna. Greensward was laid down. Soon Gehenna had become a park, and in 1978 the first gala open-air concert was held there, in celebration of Israel's thirtieth Independence Day. I had perched in a tree just below Yemin Moshe, watching excitedly as a mass of humanity flowed into what had once been no-man's-land. I could look far down into the concert bowl, or up through the leaves as the stars came out, or far out down the valley into the blackness of the desert night. It was a splendid seat. Zubin Mehta was conducting, Isaac Stern and Jean-Pierre Rampal playing, Leontyne Price singing. The climax, as in all such concerts, was meant to be the *1812* Overture, fireworks and all. But for me it came as I nearly fell out of the tree, swaying to Leontyne Price as she sang, "He's got the whole world in His hands."

Despite that uncertain perch, life in Yemin Moshe was no longer life on the edge. It was the center now. And the only reminder of Moloch's onetime reign over this valley was the sound of tanks rumbling through at night.

✡

Jerusalem still has a monster, to be sure, but a new and benign one. It was built in the early seventies and rises two stories high from a huge sandpit in a suburb of West Jerusalem. It is a huge lumpy sculpture by Niki de Saint-Phalle, white with big black splotches and three gigantic red tongues that spew out from its mouth and down into the sand.

Like the older monster, this one too devours children. They swarm up the steps around its back and into its cavelike mouth, then slide down the tongues into the sand, screaming and wriggling all the way. The bravest go headfirst. All over the city, parents get children to eat their spinach by saying "If you don't, you can't go play on the Monster today."

The children have marked out the Monster as their own, and resent adult infringement on their territory. If you are over twelve years old, you can only go there after their bedtime, as I did late one cold winter night with an old friend from abroad. He was in Jerusalem on a brief visit, and I was showing him the city.

As we went up the steps, snowflakes began to drift through the air. It was cold inside the mouth. We crouched there

9

watching the slow swirl of crystals and huddled against each other for warmth. And then for more than that. Perhaps we would have done so in any case, later, inside four walls. Or perhaps it was simply the place itself that could not be resisted. Whichever, we made love in the mouth of the Monster, and afterward slid down the tongues into the sand and the snow.

These are the ways you make a city your own. You walk, work, love, separate, laugh, cry, argue and dance in it. You go to funerals and to weddings in it. You shiver and sweat, hurt and heal in it until every part of it becomes "a place where" — where this happened, where that was said. You live in a city until it becomes inseparable from your life.

I had been away five years now, yet the city still claimed me. As the moon moved above me that first night back at Mishkenot, Jerusalem seemed like a passionate love affair that had lasted beyond its time but would not break. Everything that pulled me toward it had a dark side that pushed me away. I knew this, but it was hard to remember that dark side on this night, as the lone dog still howled and a faint breeze rose, rustling the berries of the Persian lilac tree.

Now I was a visitor in what had once been my home. Now I hoped to resolve this passion of mine — to find a cooler, more detached view of this city and this country. I knew "on my flesh," as the Hebrew phrase puts it, that this was a place where the personal and the political blend and intertwine — where the one affects, informs and deepens the other, making politics intensely personal and the personal, inevitably, political. But I thought that by going to the roots of this passion, I could find some sort of equilibrium, and thus make my peace with this place. By returning to the beginning, I could find the thread that would lead me to the end.

At the end, I thought, I would finally break the thread, knot it, and leave.

As my moon shadow lengthened on the flagstones, the span of years contracted again. I was back only a few hours, yet it felt as though I had never left. I might still be twenty, still innocent of war and conflict, terrorism and hate. I felt utterly peaceful.

"What am I doing here? I thought I'd left," I said to myself again. And then, with a smile, "But how could I leave this place?"

Seduced by beauty, I had forgotten the danger it contained.

II

THE missile attack came that Sunday afternoon.
There had been explosions all morning, echoing loud and long through the hills, but they were just sonic booms. Tourists ducked for cover on Jaffa Road as Israelis demonstratively walked on unperturbed, recognizing the sounds for what they were. The booms rattled windows, shook doors and reverberated from hill to hill. In Safed, six schoolchildren were cut by shattered glass. In Jerusalem, only the peace of the morning was shattered.

Once, there had been no planes at all over Jerusalem. Until 1967, it had been out of bounds, on the border; after that, the air force had all of Sinai over which to practice its diving, turning, spinning, and strafing runs. But the Sinai went back to Egypt in 1981, and the air force was forced back into the skies over Israel's cities. The sonic booms have become an everyday matter, yet they are still unsettling. When there are no tourists around, Israelis allow themselves to look upward worriedly; the sound reminds them that an explosion is always possible.

The planes are the ironic modern counterpart to the medieval kabbalists' idea of the two Jerusalems: *Yerushalayim shel maala,* the higher, heavenly Jerusalem, and *Yerushalayim shel mata,* the lower, earthly one. Easy to understand why the kabbalists needed two. Looking at the sewage-strewn alleys and the impoverished population of those times, they said to themselves that this could not be. Jerusalem was a holy city. Therefore there must be another city, a higher one, a shining heavenly one to balance this all-too-earthly one that dirtied their shoes and assaulted their nostrils. They made Jerusalem schizophrenic.

By early afternoon, the planes were turning back to base. They reached from earth to heaven in one steep climb, then glinted in the sunlight as they streaked out of sight. Beneath them, I walked along the hillside from Yemin Moshe, on my way to see Dennis Silk, poet and puppet-master, who is something of an expert on the two Jerusalems. Jerusalemites treasure his book *Retrievements,* an anthology of writings on the city — from the early kabbalists to present-day cynics — that veers crazily from love to hate, enchantment to contempt, as each writer saw either heaven or earth. Dennis is one of those who sees both.

He lives high above the city on the hill of Abu Tor, inside the walls of the Greek Orthodox Compound: a few stone houses scattered among wind-bent pines, a field of thorns and weeds with a giant saltbush spreading over them, and a commanding view of Mount Zion and Yemin Moshe, the gold and silver domes of the mosques, and the desert beyond.

In the center of the compound is the old stone bandstand. First the Turkish and then the British army bands used to play here on weekends, trumpet voluntaries sounding out across the desert hills. Now only the sounds of the city waft up the hill, muffled by height and distance. This is the old, neglected Jerusalem, run-down and gone to seed. A place for lovers, and for poets.

Dennis too has taken on something of that benign neglect: bushy eyebrows arching over a gently chiseled face, gray hair thinning as he moves through his fifties but always wild, flying away from his head at a different angle each time I see him. The walls of his house are papered with his own collection of retrievements. There are the bright primary colors of religious posters: Two Abrahams sacrifice an Isaac and an Ishmael, side by side, one in Hebrew and the other in Arabic, while Mohammed's winged horse El-Barak leaps twice over the black stone of Mecca on its night flight to Jerusalem. In one poster El-Barak has the curly blond head of a Marilyn Monroe, and in the other the luscious dark curls of a Jane Russell. Then there are Javanese shadow puppets and faded posters of puppet plays, a firing-range dummy found near the Central Bus Station, paintings and drawings by various friends, and everywhere, books. It is another world up here on the hill of Abu Tor, gentle and worn like Dennis's face — a world of sighs and quirks, of sudden insights and slow rumination.

Until 1967 the border ran right through Abu Tor, just below Dennis's house. It divided a village into two countries, and thus preserved it. "This neighborhood really had a vested interest in war," said Dennis as we sat by the open door, watching the pines rustle in the breeze. "I think it's only war that kept it going like this for so long."

I was shocked to hear him say that. Not because it was untrue, but because I realized that I too had that vested interest in war. Most of the neighborhoods I loved in Jerusalem had been border areas, too close to danger for the developers. Nearly all of them had succumbed to architects' plans since 1967. This compound was one of the last holdouts.

"It's surprising we've lasted until now when you think of it," Dennis was saying. "Every few months in the last few years I've seen contractors come here. You can tell them by their voices and the way they stand on the bandstand, sizing it all up. Hard, chunky people. They always went away again. But this time, it looks like this is it.''

This time, one of the partners of the main contractor was a former finance minister under Menachem Begin. The plans and the permits had all been pushed through. The city planners had fought a delaying action, trying to hold down the damage, but they couldn't prevent the project altogether; the Greek Orthodox Church had a right to sell, and the contractors a right to build. So within the year, the compound would no longer exist. A brand-new hotel would rise where the saltbush now stood, Dennis's house would disappear, and an underground passage for tourist buses would be blasted through the rock beneath the bandstand. ''Maybe the saltbush will rot them out,'' said Dennis vehemently.

We abandoned the subject, and examined his collection of old mechanical toys. Tin bicyclists and motorists tinkled around in tight circles on the patchwork-tiled floor, Happy Days banners flying from their tiny masts. A Santa Claus danced slowly on a drum, the music poignantly stretched through time as the mechanism strained against age. ''A very meditative Santa,'' said Dennis, nodding slowly.

But as we watched the toys run circles on the floor, another Jerusalem began to assert itself, just a few hundred yards away.

A young man who was born the year I came to Jerusalem — the same month, in fact — crept down through the carefully planted bushes just twenty yards from my doorway at Mishkenot. He had lived the same time as I in this city. The same, yet very different.

His name was David Ben-Shimol. His parents came to Israel from Morocco in the early fifties. After some time in an immigrant camp, and after the automatic delousing and other indignities dealt to North African immigrants, they found themselves in Jerusalem — not my Jerusalem, but a jerry-built new suburb that rapidly developed into a slum. He was one of eleven children growing up in poverty. Resentment became his raison d'être, and out of it grew hate.

As Dennis and I talked of the wild beauty of the old Jerusalem, Ben-Shimol nursed his LAW antitank missile in his arms. He had been AWOL from the army for a few days now, and had stolen the missile from his base. He had no doubts about what he was going to do. He was going to be a hero. Break out of the cycle of poverty and neglect. Be famous, like the ultranationalist messianic Gush Emunim men who had formed the Jewish terror network in the West Bank. They had blown the legs off two Arab mayors and gunned down students in an Islamic seminary. Then they had planned to blow up the mosques in Jerusalem and obliterate those gold and silver domes. They were in jail now, to be sure, but they were being treated like national heroes by half the country. Cabinet ministers were pressing for special conditions for them, saying what good boys they were, and how they had only done what had to be done in defense of their families. It never occurred to Ben-Shimol that blowing up people helped defend nobody's family. Anything against the Arabs was fine. Especially after Cremisan.

That had been the week before. Two Jewish hikers had been walking in a wadi near the Cremisan Monastery, just outside Bethlehem. An Arab guard working at a nearby Israeli building site stole a rifle, followed them down into the wadi, tied them up, tortured them, and killed them. The press had duly reported all the reactions: Gush Emunim leaders calling for revenge, right-wing Knesset members calling for revenge, the man in the street calling for revenge.

The Arab guard was known in his village as touched in the

head, and had a long record, dating back to Jordanian times, of mad and near-suicidal actions. But neither the Knesset members nor David Ben-Shimol were interested in that. An Arab had killed Jews. Therefore revenge must be taken. And since nobody else seemed about to take it, since the heroes of Gush Emunim were in jail, Ben-Shimol would take on the mission himself. He would exact the right revenge: two Arabs for every Jew.

He had with him the letter to leave behind once he had done his task. It was in his best handwriting, in red ballpoint pen. It was also full of spelling mistakes, but he didn't know that. He headed the page with *Basad,* the acronym for *BeSiyata DeShimaya,* "with the help of heaven," the Aramaic phrase used by Orthodox Jews to head anything they write. It was odd, since Ben-Shimol was not Orthodox. "In revenge for Cremisan," he had written. "Two Arabs to be killed for every Jew. The Jewish underground to be freed. The death sentence to be given to the Cremisan murderer."

He waited for a bus — an "Arab bus," as it was later described in the press, as though ethnicity were an attribute of inanimate objects. Easy to tell the Arab buses from the "Jewish" ones (though nobody ever talks of Jewish buses; they use the name of the firm, Egged, instead): they were old and noisy and multicolored, like the posters on Dennis's walls. And besides, Egged buses hardly used this route. It was an Arab route, avoiding the center of Jewish West Jerusalem.

There were plenty of buses straining up the hill out of Gehenna, on their way to the Bethlehem and Hebron roads, but Ben-Shimol needed one that was going particularly slowly. The LAW missile was a tricky business. He had had a little training in using it, and knew it was not nearly so good as the Americans claimed. They said it was accurate up to two hundred and fifty yards, but in fact you had to be closer. Far closer. And it had a tendency to fire upward, so you had to aim low.

It was close to three in the afternoon when he saw the right bus. It was older than the others, its colors faded, its engine complaining on the incline. He crept down a bit lower, readied the missile, and waited for the bus to come level with him. He was ten yards from the road.

✡

You never forget the sound. That instant recognition never leaves you. There is something short and sharp and horribly final about it. And a flat silence the moment after.

I looked quickly at Dennis. "That's an explosion."

He nodded. "I'm afraid you're right."

We went outside. I looked first to the east. "The mosques are still there," I said, knowing this for false reassurance. An attack on the mosques would have made far more noise. I knew this was something much smaller. And I also knew it was deadly.

Within a minute or so, the sirens began. More and more of them tore into the air, building to a crescendo of urgency and panic as ambulances drove wildly to the scene, blaring past lines of stalled cars. From our hilltop vantage point, we found their focus down there on the slope, just beneath my door. We stood and watched helplessly, knowing that if we went on down the police would turn us away. A few minutes later, the ambulances began to drive off, their sirens fading into the distance like the howls of jackals in the night before they begin to feed. In the new silence, a single hawk glided on the air currents above Gehenna, turning large lazy circles alone against the clear blue sky.

One man was killed. Ten people were injured. Despite Ben-

Shimol's training, the missile had gone high, cutting into the bus just below the roof instead of through the center. If it had worked as he intended, at least twenty people would have been killed.

He was arrested five days later. He was very proud of himself. According to Southern District Police Commander Avraham Turgeman (replaced some months later after a bribery scandal), his motives were "emotional, nationalistic and Jewish." It was left to others to ask what "Jewish motives" might be, or how come they included murder.

Ben-Shimol's fantasies of glory were disappointed. Nobody called him "good but misguided" or "an excellent boy" as they had the Gush Emunim terrorists. Nobody graced him with the softer phrase "underground fighter." In *Ha'aretz*, Israel's leading paper, columnist Bet Michael let loose with bitter sarcasm: Ben-Shimol was just a petty criminal from the slums, not one of the government-sponsored elite on the West Bank. He was a poor dumb kid from a Jerusalem backwater, not a heroic pioneer making the West Bank "Jewish." "He hasn't talked with the messiah, he hasn't studied with the Rav Kook. . . . And because he's not a graduate of the right yeshiva, he's just an ugly stain dirtying the purity of the underground."

The only one to publicly claim Ben-Shimol was the openly fascistic Meir Kahane, the American-born rabbi and Knesset member. Kahane called him a brave hero and paid his court expenses. Gush Emunim, Techiya and other right-wing groups supporting the "underground" relaxed. Their motives remained respectable by comparison, fostered in government-sponsored settlements and yeshivas and financed by taxes and contributions from abroad. If that money had been spent on welfare and education, Ben-Shimol might have been different. But the government had ignored him all of his eighteen years, and continued to do so now. Nobody in the cabinet asked for clemency for him as they did for the Gush Emunim killers. He got no leave to join his family on holidays, and no special privileges in jail. He had no connections.

The morning after his attack, I sat on the terrace of Mishkenot, reading the papers and watching the police measure and mark the ground nearby. These dwellings were no longer tranquil. Sweet memories of innocence had been trampled by the present, by blood and racism and hatred.

Not that any of this was new. But when the blood was still fresh on the ground so close to where I sat, when it hadn't yet been washed away by rain, there was no longer any room for illusions of innocence.

Ben-Shimol had brought me back to a painful reality. To be sure, it was beautiful here, and that beauty was haunting — a mystic world of legend and clear light, the higher Jerusalem. But the lower Jerusalem was literally one of flesh and blood. Torn flesh and spilled blood. And that makes it the real Jerusalem.

A familiar bitterness welled up inside me. It was the bitterness of despair. Jerusalem is *Yerushalayim* in Hebrew, from *Ir Shalem,* "city of peace." But it has never been a city of peace. It has been, and still is, the most fought-for city in the world, and the most conquered. Go down to the excavations by the southern wall of the Temple Mount, beneath the El-Aqsa mosque, and you can see the layers of conquering civilizations, one literally on top of the other: a Hasmonean cellar, a Herodian storeroom, a Roman bathroom, a Byzantine house, an Ottoman palace, a Crusader wall, a Turkish wall . . . Each civilization was built on the ruins of the preceding one.

It occurred to me now that I might be on a fool's quest: one cannot make peace with a country at war, nor look for equilibrium in a place of constant crisis. I looked over at Mount Zion, at the greenery, the neat stone walls winding round the side of the hill, the dome of the Dormition Abbey rising gently into the sky. I had never left this Jerusalem, the one of legend and light, the universal Jerusalem. Nobody could. We carry it in our minds, even if we have never set foot in the city. It was Ben-Shimol's Jerusalem that I had left, exhausted by this welling of despair and hopelessness, by this terrible feeling of inevitability as I watched hatred and racism build on resentment and fanaticism in an ages-old cycle of violence.

Yet the two Jerusalems are connected. As Dennis said, we have a vested interest in war. A city holy to three religions can never be peaceful. It means too much to too many people. And that is part of the excitement of it, and part of its beauty. If Mount Zion were called Mount Monadnock, say, or Mount Apple, or by any other name except perhaps for Sinai, Ararat or Everest, it would not seem so entrancing. The two Jerusalems depend on each other, as they always have. And we who live here are trapped between them.

III

EVERYWHERE I went, there were welcomes. And every welcome became a challenge.

The creases on Yehuda's face lifted as he held me at arm's length before giving me another hug. "You're so happy and bubbly, it's wonderful," he said. "We've forgotten what it's like to be that way here." He paused a moment and frowned. "Maybe you shouldn't stay too long, or it will happen to you too."

Tsiona was in the pharmacy, waiting as the two women in front of her argued about whose turn it was to be served. Her face opened wide in a smile as she greeted me, then closed again as the argument in front of her became louder. "What a mess this country has become," she said, long dark hair shaking around her shoulders. "It's good for you that you're not living here anymore."

The clerk in the post office looked up and smiled over her half-glasses as she totted up columns of figures. She'd seen me through a crisis or two, including the time I'd walked in accompanied by a policeman who had come to my door threatening to take me to jail unless I paid my parking tickets of the past two years in his presence. She'd laughed then. (So had the policeman.) Now she said wryly: "Pity you left."

Moshe and Lea left a note for me at Mishkenot. "Welcome home," it said. "Oh no," I thought, uncomfortable at this blatant attempt to pull me back in. "They've got it wrong. I'm just a visitor now."

I stopped in to see Morele in his office. His face seemed more creased than ever under the prematurely white hair, a legacy of the Yom Kippur War. He was in khaki, and grimaced when I told him he looked good in it. I'd been lucky to catch him; though in reserve service, he'd just stopped into the office to see to a couple of cases due in court the next week. Lawyers can never stop working. "What'll I tell you?" he said. "I'm glad for me that you're here. But for you?" He shrugged. "That's not for me to say." He had been one of those who had done their best to persuade me not to leave.

Ruthy in the government press office peered at me as though I had landed from some alien planet when I turned down her offer for a journalist's junket to Lebanon. "I don't understand," she said. "If you're not doing an article on Lebanon, then why come back?"

The owner of the newspaper store on Jaffa Road greeted me as though I'd only been out of town for a week. His eyes sparkled with pleasure behind his round glasses. "Of course you're back," he said. "This is where you feel at home. Now all we need to do is find a good young man to keep you here." I laughed. "Oh no, don't laugh. These things are important. You belong here; you just need someone to make you realize that."

"How long are you here for?" asked Ami cautiously as he drew up alongside me at a stoplight. He'd put on weight. I noticed he was wearing a yarmulke. "Are you here to stay, or just to visit?" The lights turned green and the honking of cars behind us drowned out my answer. "I'll call," he yelled as he revved his engine and went speeding on over the intersection.

Gadi saw me in the supermarket, and his loud voice suddenly boomed at my back: "Well, well, so you're here again. You should come back for good. We could do with some more sane voices around here." People turned to look at this paragon of sanity. Gadi ignored them. His tone of voice betrayed no expectation that I would come back. He talked about leaving himself, "just for a year or two." I had also left just for a year or two . . .

"You have to come back," said Annie, the photographer. We had met in line at the bank, then gone for coffee. She had come straight to Palestine from the concentration camps after World War II, and maybe because of that, or because she was a wise woman in any case, I always listened carefully to her. I admired her certainty, and asked why she was so sure. "Because you're a Jerusalemite," she said. "And what I'm telling you now is not true for people from other cities, only from Jerusalem. It's because when a Jerusalemite leaves, it's like taking a stone out of a wall. There's a hole there, where you were. Waiting for you to come fill it again."

✡

I looked myself up in the phone book. I was still listed, even though I'd sold the house three years before. I felt perversely pleased.

Not that the telephone is even necessary in Jerusalem. Within a few days, I had seen most of the people I would have called anyway. I saw them in the street, the cafés, the bank, the stores — the chance meetings of a small town, which Jerusalem still is, despite the doubling of its population since 1967. There were so many people I was glad to see again. So many with whom I had a casual depth of friendship that is hard to find anywhere else in the world. Sometimes, I remembered,

24

it felt as though I could stretch out my arms and touch the whole city, as once I had stood on a hilltop outside Jerusalem and stretched out my arms beneath the Milky Way until it seemed as though I were holding the whole arc of it, the stars pouring from one palm into the other to make me into some celestial conjurer.

I was not a wraith in the streets here as I was in New York, where everyone deliberately looks through everyone else, afraid to let eyes meet. I could feel myself coming alive again under the sun, as though I had been too long indoors. It was good to be welcomed and accepted back, to feel part of the place again, a piece of the wall. Yet even as it happened, I wondered if it could still be true. "Being back is both wonderful and terrible," I wrote on postcards to friends in the States. "Paradox, paradox, all is paradox." I realized only much later that I had written the words of a resident, not of a visitor: not "being here" but "being back."

The truth is that I felt at home in this place I was determined to leave. Home is not just a physical place where you can imagine yourself in the future. It is a state of mind. It is where you feel part of the place. Where you feel involved, loved, known, accepted. Where you are inside. And where you live the strange double life of talking differently to insiders than to outsiders.

At a dinner party in Tel Aviv some years before, there had been a visiting American academic who was part of a "fact-finding mission" designed to make a full study of the political situation in the quixotic span of ten days. It may not have been surprising that he should burst out in frustration, but it was the way he did it that riled me. "The trouble with you Israelis," he said, "is that you seem to enjoy living in an armed camp. What's the matter with you people? Are you trying to bring down another Holocaust around your heads?"

I had asked something similar myself, with friends. But to this man we were "you people." Solutions came easy to him; he was safely outside. Instead of pain, struggle and conflict, he felt only impatience and a scornful antagonism. I argued with him all evening.

Not long after that, one of Israel's top journalists had been asked by an American magazine to write an article called "Has Israel Lost Its Soul?" He turned down the assignment. "Why?" someone asked. "You've been saying it often enough in the Hebrew press." He gave a despairing shrug: "I can't. It's read differently in the States. Knowing that, I'd only end up writing an apologia."

We find ourselves backed into a false position. Reacting to the black-and-white picture seen by those who sit at a distance, we hear ourselves defending positions we would normally attack. We balk when the words come from others who are not part of the "we," who do not care in any personal way, but simply judge. And the main reason for this, I suspect, is shame. Home is also the place that can shame you.

Every day, the world news offers up its portion of religious fanaticism and vigilantism at work, of killings in the streets and corruption in the governments. I react with the disgust and indignation of any decent person anywhere. But when that news comes from Israel, something deep inside me breaks apart a little more, as though I were responsible.

The usual answers — "Israel is no worse than any other country . . . It's far better than the Arab countries . . . Think what they would do if the positions were reversed" — are self-justifying platitudes. Iran and Syria are not my standards of behavior. And though we complain of the world's double standard for Israel and the Arab countries, we should remember that Israel itself has helped promote this double standard of expectation. It may burden Israelis, but it also makes them proud.

Israel may be the only country in the world of which one asks "Has it lost its soul?" — or which asks itself that question. As it does. *Heshbon nefesh* is the "accounting of the soul" done on Yom Kippur, the Day of Atonement. It is not confession as in Catholicism, but an inner dialogue with conscience that affords no absolution. And since the Yom Kippur War in 1973, it has been part of the political vocabulary. The soul-searching done after that war — "Where is Israel going? What's happening to us?" — never reached any conclusion. The press called for *heshbon nefesh* again after the Sabra and Shatila massacres in Beirut in 1982, and yet again after the arrest of the Jewish terror network in 1984. But the irony was that only the secular responded to this religious idea. Those most impervious to a reexamination of national values were those who had committed much of the violence. And they were religious.

The country is now deeply divided. A struggle is going on inside it for power, for influence — for its soul. The democratic and humanistic concepts on which it was founded are wavering in the face of a growing tolerance for violence, messianism and contempt for the law. As Israel swings to the right, as the religious impose more on the secular, as force overpowers reason, a sense of despair has spread among those who once held the middle ground. The sense of "we" is breaking up. And with it, for many, the sense of home.

✡

Friday lunchtime in the Tsrif. The name means "the hut," and that's basically what it is: glass and wood struts holding

27

up an aging tile roof that in turn seems to support two far more aged pine trees, in an old section just off Jaffa Road. Everybody knows everybody here, and it's easy to table-hop. Nobody comes to eat lunch, except for the odd tourist. They come, newspapers bunched under their arms, to find each other, to relax, and to commiserate about "the situation."

This Friday, Dennis Silk was at one table sparring phrases with fellow poet and dramatist Arieh Sachs. Morele sat at another, providing a friendly ear for a fellow lawyer in the process of divorce. The place was comfortingly the same: rough serviceable tables surrounded by a variety of wooden chairs, tiny bunches of flowers stuck in jam jars on the tables, the rustle of newspapers, hum of voices, smells of coffee, wine and cigarettes. Oded pulled an extra chair to the journalists' table for me, and the circle around it shifted to expand. Here, gathered like King Arthur's knights, were the best and the brightest of the country's younger journalists, bouncing their frustrations off each other with humor that gets so black it can be hard to laugh.

Oded is no longer so young, but he was the first and the sharpest of this generation, and the most romantic behind his cynicism. He was riding the wave of an idea. Somebody had read out a report of Deputy Premier Yitzhak Shamir's loud dismissal of new signs of moderation within the Palestine Liberation Organization. Oded mockingly adopted a grave face, shook his head as a doctor might at a hopeless case, and lowered his voice to a regretful medical tone: "Another case of paxophobia."

Paxophobia, it turned out, was an irrational fear of peace. While the patient declaims his desire for peace all the time, any actual sign of peace in the offing sends him into hysteria: his eyes glass over, he foams at the mouth, he refuses to listen to another word. There are paranoid tendencies — peace is seen as a threat to the patient's identity, therefore to be rejected at all costs. And aggressive tendencies too — the patient is liable to attack anyone he sees as a peace provocateur, and can cause grievous bodily harm. "So far as we know at this stage of medical science, the disease is incurable," Oded concluded with a look of mournful irony.

"No hope?" someone asked. "Only one," he replied, "and that's that so far as we can tell, paxophobia is not hereditary."

At first it had been funny, but by now it wasn't anymore, and the subject changed. Such ideas don't last too long around this table. When you hide your pain with humor, it doesn't always work. Sometimes the satire veers so close to reality that it is no longer humor, but more like a particularly bitter truth.

"Ah well, who'd be a doctor?" said Oded, turning to me. "If I had my choice now, I'd grow grapes. Champagne grapes. In Italy. I'd become a gentleman farmer." The image of this lean intellectual pruning vines in Tuscany was irresistibly incongruous. "Don't laugh," he said. "I wish I *could* change my profession." His thick tortoiseshell glasses slipped down the bridge of his nose as he reverted to seriousness. "I want to give up my column. There's nothing left for me to write. I've called these politicians every name it's possible to call them. But no matter how bad things get, they always seem to get worse. I have no language for it anymore. I'm just saying the same things over and over again."

I objected. I'd miss his biting critiques, all the stronger for the elegance of their language. "Tell him," someone else butted in. "See if you can convince him, because we can't."

There didn't seem to be much chance of convincing him. "Is this what it's like to live in inner exile?" he asked. "Sure, we can write whatever we want, it's just that nobody takes any notice of it. We're tolerated as a liberal fringe in a society that's moved way off to the right. So why write if it makes no difference?" He took an absentminded sip from my wineglass. "And why write at all about leaving a country like this, like you're doing? People have always moved from one country to another. Why do we have to make such an issue of it here?"

They were rhetorical questions, and Oded knew it. True, anywhere else in the world, deciding to leave would be a personal matter, of no interest to anyone except my close friends. But here, there is no dividing line between the personal and the political. Here, it's a toss-up whether you first discuss politics and then make love, or first make love and then discuss politics. Here, personal decisions can be a matter of national prestige.

Migration figures are front-page news: not starlings flocking in the trees each fall, but people. The core of the Zionist idea is *aliya,* "going up" to Israel. Its opposite is *yerida,* "going down," and the figures for that are a poorly kept secret. The year Menachem Begin came to power, 1977, was the first year that *yerida* was higher than *aliya,* and it's been that way since. There is even a special division within the Ministry of Immigration to persuade Israelis who have left to come back, but there's an air of helplessness among those who work there, touched with envy. When an Israeli decides to emigrate, others feel that a judgment is being made on them — either on their own decision not to leave, or on their inability to do so. What you think of those who leave depends on your political point of view. They may be traitors, or weaklings, or lucky bastards who have made a break for it.

Whatever his fantasies about growing grapes, Oded wasn't leaving. "I can't. This is my material, and this is my language. What else can I do? But you, you can move. You can write about anything you like, anywhere you like. You don't need all this.''

I smiled ruefully, remembering a lunchtime conversation with a New York magazine editor some weeks before. "You'll write about other things," he'd said, "but Israel is your passion." Maybe I did need all this.

"Your problem," said Oded, irony overcoming the mournfulness, "is that you're a victim of the '67 war. If it hadn't been for that war, you'd probably have left within a year or so of coming here. Gone back and done your doctorate. Become a professor of psychology. Gone to India. Any of a thousand and one things. It was that war that kept you here. It's the same with someone like Moshe Levinger. You and Levinger, you're both victims of the same war.''

I didn't appreciate the comparison. Rabbi Moshe Levinger was one of the leaders of Gush Emunim, and had apparently been involved in the terrorist plan to blow up the mosques. But Oded was warming to his theme: "If it hadn't been for '67 — if we hadn't conquered the West Bank and given Levinger his chance to create a biblical return to the Greater Israel — what would he be doing today? He'd probably be selling shoelaces in Petah Tikva.'' It was a calculated insult. "You and Levinger, both victims of the same war,'' he repeated, then sat back and finished my wine with a look of satisfaction at a circle neatly closed.

It was not the first time I had been compared to Moshe Levinger. A few years before, I had been attacked by a columnist in the *Jewish Week,* a national American newspaper. The occasion of the attack was my description of Levinger in a magazine article: "an ascetic-looking man with yellowish pallor, bad teeth and a voice that rarely descends from hysteria.'' The columnist had hastened to assure her readers that

Levinger's teeth were not so bad, and that in any case the quality of teeth and the quality of political wisdom were not connected. Richard Nixon had wonderful teeth, and some Gush Emunim leaders were as handsome as movie stars. And besides, she pointed out, you could tell a lot from the quality of my own teeth, which she had seen flashing in a wide grin on the back of a book jacket. It was quite possible that "gorgeous teeth like those draw some vital element out of the Jewish mind and soul."

I swallowed the insult, clipped the article, and sent it to the orthodontist who had treated me as a child. Trying to persuade me to accept braces, he had told me that when I was older, people would comment on my excellent teeth. The argument made little sense to a ten-year-old, yet here it had come to fruition — with a fickle twist he never intended.

Now I was being compared again to Levinger, but from the other side of the conflict, my own side. Fate was getting mean as well as fickle. "So many victims of that war, then," I said to Oded. "Levinger, me, David Ben-Shimol — all of us. If you look at it that way, we're all victims of that war."

"Not I," he said determinedly. "That was never my war. I argued against it solidly for a month before it happened."

"Then you were victimized all the more by it," I retorted, angry at the idea of being a victim. But part of that anger was the knowledge that Oded might be right. I might indeed have left then, in 1967, if there had been no war.

IV

THAT year before the '67 war, the city was still small. The stars were larger and more plentiful and shinier — not because I remember them that way, but because Jerusalem was smaller and darker. Bedouin still herded goats and sheep across the main roads from stony field to stony hillside, leaving trails of droppings to dry in the early-morning sun. There were no traffic fumes on Jaffa Road; there was not enough traffic. And the border, which defined the life of the city, barely existed in the minds of those who lived there.

We simply did not see the border. Because it was so close, it was not quite real. Or we couldn't afford to think of its reality. We saw its symbols, to be sure: the fire walls and the concrete antitank dragons' teeth, the barbed wire and the signs. CAUTION: BORDER AREA. WARNING: NO-MAN'S-LAND. DANGER: MINES. But we didn't see what made the border real, what defined it: the other side.

Less than a hundred yards separated us from Jordan, yet for us that hundred yards could have been a thousand miles. The border defined the limits of our vision. We adjusted our eyesight to it, and became shortsighted.

Only after the war, when I came home to find a single bullet lodged in my living-room wall, did I realize that I could see Jaffa Gate from there. It was one of the main gates into the Old City. I stared hard, trying to remember what I had seen before. Had there been ruined houses in front of it, or trees? Or had something less tangible blinded me? I only knew that a week before, I hadn't even been aware that the gate was there. It was pointless to see what was beyond reach, to look where you couldn't go. How else could we live with the fact that a forbidden distant country was just a five-minute walk away?

The border didn't worry me at all. I was at the start of my adult life, and since it was the sixties and times were different then everywhere in the world, I gave no thought to where I was going or what I would do with my life. To be twenty at that time meant that experience was all.

In any case, I was still fresh from the English ban-the-bomb movement and the Aldermaston marches. I was convinced that the only war I would ever see would be the big one, the nuclear one, the third world war. I had no idea that death could be as real by conventional as by nuclear means.

Yet in the weeks before June 5, 1967, even I began to realize that war was imminent. Nasser closed the Straits of Tiran, and in Israel men were called up into the army reserves. I filled sandbags and folded bandages along with other civilians. We listened to the Jordanian radio. Bagpipes floated eerily over the airwaves as though from another time, calling Jordanian soldiers to war. Huge mobs in Cairo called for all the Jews to be thrown into the sea.

Each morning I would wake, look out through the arch of the window to the deepening blue of the sky, and think: "The sun is shining — there can't be a war today."

The sun was shining the morning of June 5, too.

At eight in the morning, the all-clear siren sounded. Nobody knew why. I went to work in the publishing house where

I was an editor. At eleven, the Jordanians began to shell. We sat in the basement listening to the bombardment. All the shells were coming in; none were going out.

We couldn't move out into the streets to get anyone home; the shelling was too heavy. Mothers panicked and wives groaned. I was in love again by then, and he was at the front, but I lacked the sense to worry. It didn't occur to me that one of us could be killed and the other not.

I don't remember just when the lull came. I do remember driving people home, a frantic race against an undefined time limit lest the shelling start again. When it did, I was on the last leg — racing home with friends to stay at their house, since mine, on the border, offered no safety at all.

At least now we could hear shells going out as well as coming in. We sped down the road as shells landed close by, throwing up fountains of earth and stone. I began zigzagging crazily to avoid them. "It's just like in the movies," I thought.

Later, I discovered that many soldiers in the front line thought the same thing. A basic defense mechanism: It's not real. It's just a movie. These shells can't hurt me. "Every shell has a name on it," they say in the army, "and either it's yours or it's not." Chance. Nothing you can do about it. The bottom line was another saying: "What about the shell addressed 'To whom it may concern'?"

The same peculiar thinking made me park over a small crater where a shell had just exploded: if one had already landed there, another wouldn't. By the time we reached shelter, I was strangely unconcerned. For the next day and a half, we listened nonstop to the radio. We watched at night as flares and shells lit up the sky to the east, on the hills around the Old City. We heard the news that the Egyptian air force had been destroyed, and that Israeli forces were in the Sinai, in Hebron, in the Old City. Hope became wonder, wonder became realization. This was not the end; we would not be thrown into the sea; we were winning.

The war began on a Monday. By the Wednesday, it was over in Jerusalem. That afternoon, Moshe Dayan, Yitzhak Rabin and Levi Eshkol — the defense minister, chief of staff and prime minister — went to the Wailing Wall. I went with my friends up to the old border, near the Russian Compound. And it was then that my defenses crumbled. Then, for the first time, I really acknowledged what war meant.

It wasn't the bullet marks on the walls, or the smashed windows, or the craters in the ground. It wasn't the sudden talk of pulling down the Mandelbaum Gate checkpoint between the two halves of the city, or of going to the Wailing Wall. It wasn't the euphoria of having won. No. It was the soldiers. The young men, my age, sitting slumped against the walls of houses, their helmets off, the marks where their goggles had been making white eyes against dusty blackened skin, their guns thrown beside them on the pavement, their legs awry as they lay in exhaustion. It was their faces. The look on their faces, in their eyes. The look that was half exhaustion, half shock. The look of young men — boys — who had come back from hand-to-hand fighting through the alleys of the Old City. The look of boys who had killed. And seen their friends killed.

There was no terrible beauty being born here, as the Irish poet thought. A terrible knowledge, yes. Beauty, no. These soldiers hadn't been heroized yet. The photo of a paratrooper crying at the Wall, helmet in hand, had not yet been published. The casualty figures not yet released. The medals not yet given. There was only the knowledge of what they had done: the blood, the cordite, the smoke, the fire, and the fear.

Days passed. Between the fear and the glory, it was no contest. The euphoria of victory took over. My friend came back from the front, head swathed in bandages. I was walking home from work, he was walking down the hill. I ran to him, he opened his arms, he caught me up and swung me around and held me close. People gathered around and applauded as he kissed me. It was just like in the movies, all over again. Did I cry? I don't think so. There was no room for tears. I'd only been in the country a year. Nobody close to me had been killed. I didn't go to any military funerals. Not that war. Like everyone else, I thought I'd never have to go to one in the future either. Now we had conquered territory, and we could give it back for peace.

Well, but even the wisest of us were innocent then.

✡

Dan was among the wisest. I had known him a long time before we really began to talk to each other, as can happen in Jerusalem. By then I too was a journalist. I would see him at parties, in the government press office, at news briefings. I liked his questions. He went persistently after the facts, and politely refused to tolerate bullshit. He was a man who had fought more wars than any one man had a right to fight and survive, a man known for his toughness, both physical and mental. But there were too many stories of his exploits for him to be quite real. It was a comfort, then, that he was what he himself called "homely." That made him human. A little taller than I, he wore thick glasses perched on the end of a long curving nose, and his face was so creased that he looked far older than his late fifties. Yet he moved with the grace of a man at ease in his body. His voice was deep and warm, even caressing, and he had that way of talking that made you feel you were the only other person in a crowded room. He was irresistible to women. I have stood beside him at a cocktail party and listened as he seduced someone in five minutes, extracting a promise from her to call. Inevitably, she called the next day.

He ran a constant battle for journalistic integrity. That meant keeping a sense of responsibility in what is basically an absurd job. Some call it a profession for overgrown children. It's exciting, even heady. A certain self-importance creeps up on you from being constantly a few hours ahead of the published news. It can easily go to your head, as though you were creating the news, not reporting it.

It certainly went to one foreign journalist's head. I'll call him Chuck Cayman: a plump midwesterner in his early twenties whose continual shortness of breath — aggravated by long fat cigars in keeping with his idea of how a foreign correspondent should look — made him seem much older. I watched him on a May day in 1974 when the news came through that schoolchildren were being held hostage by terrorists in a development town in the Galilee. The town was Maalot. There was near panic in the government press office as correspondents crowded each other out of the way trying to find out where the hell Maalot was. I stood nearby, guilty for feeling thankful that the attack had not come five kilometers to the west, where friends lived on a kibbutz. Phrases floated out of the pack. "Christ, we gotta get out of here quick. If we don't get there soon it'll all be over." "ABC have already left with a camera crew from Tel Aviv, for Chrissake." "Why the hell can't the press office lay on a helicopter for us?"

Chuck emerged from the center of the fray, practically bouncing with excitement. "It's terrible," he puffed at me, "just terrible. A school full of kids, boy. . . . Hope I got enough film." I had the horrible feeling that if there'd been nobody there to see, he'd have been grinning at the thought of the bylines he'd get in the next day's papers back home.

Dan was the one to stop Chuck in his tracks. Not during Maalot, but a year later, when an old refrigerator left on the sidewalk of Jerusalem's Zion Square proved to be packed with explosives. A friend was killed in that attack. She was an immigrant from South America, and she supported the idea of an independent Palestinian state. "What a stupid way to go," I kept thinking at the funeral. "How absurd that they should kill the very Israelis who agree with them." (Many years later, I would think even that death less absurd than getting killed for a pair of roller skates or a gold neck chain in New York.)

Dan was close by when the refrigerator exploded. He remembered it in the peculiar cinematic detail with which one registers violence. The split second of silence before the blast — a moment you can never be quite sure existed in reality or only in retrospect. Then the sound of it, building with terrible slowness into a loud, long boom. And then again a silence until your ears begin to register: screams, people running, and in the distance the first ambulance sirens.

The eye begins to see: shards of glass, stone fragments, shredded clothes, a crushed watch, a shoe with something still in it. Slowly you realize that the small shapeless lumps scattered about are pieces of flesh, and that the blackish stain spreading over the ground is blood. And all around you, people, and panic.

As the police cleared the way for the ambulances, Dan just stood there, looking. The front of a hardware store had been destroyed. Iron girders hung awkwardly into the street. Mangled cans of paint had split open and their contents trailed onto the sidewalk in grotesque technicolor. Inside the store, the electricity had gone. At the back, beyond the wreckage, a group of people were clustered around the counter. For a moment, it seemed absurdly mundane — customers jostling for the salesman's attention, as though the bomb had never been. Then

Dan heard Chuck Cayman's voice, harsh and eager: "Did you see anyone hanging around? What happened when it went off? What? What did you say?"

The store owner stood behind the counter, holding himself up on it. He was shivering. At each question he flinched. He managed an indistinct answer here and there, and then stared around him, eyes wide open but dazed, as though he were looking for something but had forgotten what. His forehead, hands and arms were covered with scratches. He was in shock.

Dan walked up, grabbed Chuck by the shoulder, spun him around, reared back, and gave him a massive right to the chin. Chuck went down, reached at some boxes on a shelf as he went, and ended up on the floor with nails spilling over him. Dan said nothing. Just turned around and walked out. A few months later, Chuck transferred to South Africa.

The story quickly became legend, as stories about Dan tend to. After all, he was the one who broke the news of Israel's victory in 1967. It was the scoop of the decade. Every Chuck Cayman's dream. And he did it without setting foot outside his home. His contacts called him; he trusted them, they trusted him; he went with what he had. What he had was that Israel had destroyed the Egyptian air force before it even got off the ground — in fact, before most people in Israel or Egypt even realized that the war had begun, in the early hours of that Monday morning. That was why the all-clear siren had sounded.

The rest of the world picked up the news from Dan's broadcast. Israel Radio confirmed it. As any experienced war correspondent could see, Israel had won the war before it had even started in earnest. But then few of us are seasoned war correspondents.

No two people see a war the same way. Mine was a naive civilian's war. It was the first war I had ever seen, and a discovery of numbing excitement and death. Dan's was a journalistic and military coup, a story of lightning victory with death, for once, relegated to the background. And then there was Ya'ir's war, the soldier's war. And that was very different.

✡

Ya'ir doesn't look like a soldier. Nobody does until they put on a uniform. His lean angular face has too many shadows to be conventionally good-looking. Gentle dark eyes always seem to be half smiling, half questioning, as though he were holding something back — promising yet withholding at the same time.

We had known each other since the late sixties, when we taught together at the Bezalel art school (I psychology, he environmental design). The years passed, and from time to time I wondered what would have happened if we had gotten together. But either I was with someone else, or he was, and that hovering promise had never been fulfilled.

We went separate ways, I into journalism and he into urban planning, wrestling with the multiple problems of Jerusalem's fierce burst of growth since 1967. We would see each other here and there, at a party, in the street. Occasionally we'd go for a coffee together and swap stories of what had been happening. It became one of those deep casual acquaintances that develop so easily in Jerusalem.

There was one Friday evening in the mid-seventies, at the home of mutual friends, when Ya'ir listened quietly in his usual manner. Dan had been pressed into telling the story of his 1967 scoop. There had been another war since; an aura of self-doubt had haunted the country since that Yom Kippur of 1973, and the very idea of a war that was over before it had hardly begun seemed now like a fairy tale from the distant past.

Dan was uncomfortable with the story, and brought it to an end quickly. "But the war wasn't over," Ya'ir said.

He spoke so quietly that at first nobody heard him. He repeated his words.

Dan paused. "To all intents and purposes it was," he replied. "You can't fight a war in the Sinai without air cover. Once we'd destroyed the Egyptian air force, we had full control of the air. The rest was inevitable."

"It may have been inevitable, but it wasn't over," Ya'ir insisted. The two exchanged a look. Dan knew what he meant. So did I. But it wasn't the kind of thing to be talked about in a large group of people.

Dan knew because he himself had fought, in other wars. I knew because Ya'ir had told me. About the fear behind the glory. And as he told me, the look in his eyes had been the same as that of the soldiers slumped by the walls of the Russian Compound on the third of those six days.

He had been in a commando unit in the south of Jerusalem. Their first target was the hill of Armon HaNatziv, known as Government House, where the British High Command had been before 1948 and which the United Nations High Commission had occupied since then. It was a high hill right on the border, overlooking the whole of Jerusalem. You could see the blue U.N. flag riding high in the air from all over the city, as you still can today. Probably few of the British, and even fewer of the U.N. people, knew the older name of that hill: the Hill of Evil Counsel.

The long bare ridge stretching up to Armon HaNatziv commands one of the most impressive views of the city. In war, it is also one of the most exposed places to be. Ya'ir's unit came under heavy fire the moment they left the cover of the trees and houses of nearby Talpiot. The fire came from two directions. One was a Jordanian battery in the grounds of the monastery on the Mount of Offense, not far from the Mount of Olives. The other seemed to be the compound of the U.N. High Commission. Ya'ir's unit reported that the Jordanians had taken over the well-fortified position from the U.N. The Israelis finally took the compound after two hours under constant fire.

The commanders, the journalists and eventually the whole world knew that the war was won that morning. But those doing the fighting did not. When you're in battle, you know nothing at all about what's going on. There is no large picture.

Everything's coming from all sides. You turn round and see that the person behind you has been hit and you vaguely realize that it could as easily have been you and as the medics come running up you go on, because there's nowhere else to go. It's just a mess of noise and danger. Running. Firing. Taking cover. Running. A total mess. "I was sure I wouldn't survive that day," Ya'ir said. "I was amazed when I did."

Late that night, after midnight, when the positions they had taken were filled by the battalion following after them, they brought their dead and wounded back into town. The lightly wounded were treated at the Rehavia Gymnasia, Ya'ir's old high school. There they listened for the first time to the radio. They heard the news: the Egyptian air force destroyed, the war won. And they knew that in a few hours they'd have to go back and keep on fighting.

They rested, but with little sleep. Ya'ir remembered thinking that the next day, the Tuesday, would be it. "I'd just been given a day's reprieve, that's all. The news on the radio wasn't real. What was real was the fighting we'd seen. It took two full days until we realized that the war really had been won."

He said it without bitterness, but with a kind of quiet, private disgust that the last to realize should be those most directly involved.

Yet on that Friday evening, years later, Ya'ir would not be the only one to hold his peace. Ilana was even quieter than he, sitting in a corner and listening, as though she had nothing to say. "What could I say?" she asked me later. "There they were discussing the grand scale of history. How could my war compare with that?"

She too had been on the border. But while Dan reported and Ya'ir fought, she had nursed her newborn daughter. Miri had been born on Sunday, the day before the war began. They sent mother and child home from Hadassah Hospital first thing Monday morning to keep the beds clear for what they knew was going to come. Miri was born into one Israel, and overnight was destined to grow up in another.

An anomaly of that time: in Israel, where the phones keep breaking down at the best of times, they worked all through that war. I remember calling Ilana, wishing I was there to help her. I should have stayed in the shelter, but couldn't. It was too claustrophobic. The tension of huddled figures following the war by radio in the candlelit dark was like a scene from a World War II movie, unreal and yet full of too many associations. Ilana too was meant to be in a shelter, but she kept going up to her apartment for supplies — milk and diapers for Miri and food for Bo'az, her five-year-old. (His war would come in 1982, with Lebanon; Miri's has not yet come.)

Our voices reached across the gunfire and the shelling. "Are you all okay?" "Yes, how about you?" "Okay. Did you hear from David?" David, her husband, was in the army spokesman's office. "He called. He's tired. He says we've won the war."

I knew it was true, yet with the shells still landing, it was also absurd. "Someone should tell that to the Jordanians."

"I think they're finding out the hard way. Did you hear the last news bulletin?"

"Yes, what do you think?"

As Ilana warmed the baby's milk, we discussed the latest reports like old-time generals, and then took refuge in the small practical details of disrupted lives. There was the milk I'd left out to defrost that Monday morning. There was the plant on Ilana's balcony that had been blown away by the force of a shell landing nearby. There was the question of how long her supply of clean diapers could last.

The disconnected conversations of the civilians' war: a war of transistor radios and dirty diapers, of soured milk and tempers flaring in the shelters, of the skyline lit red and orange at night by army flares, of craters suddenly appearing outside your door. (In Jerusalem it only lasted three days; how could they stand it in Beirut all these years?)

Dan, Ya'ir, Ilana, myself: four wars, each very different. Yet each the same three days in Jerusalem. Was one any more real than the others? Any more important? Any more absurd?

And then, some weeks later, a fifth war arrived in the form of a letter from a relative in England. "We're so proud of Israel now," he wrote, "and so proud that you're there. We feel we can stand straight and raise our heads as Jews." Jews all over the world seem to feel as he did. But there was no reality there for me. Wars are always more glorious when fought far away. When you can't see the fear in the faces of those who fought them. And when you don't have to live with the results of them.

V

IT was still *hamsin*. Instead of relief from the long hot summer, the earth baked and cracked even more. It was way past the time when the first rain usually falls. The weather seemed as wrong as the time. There were exactly six hundred Israeli dead in Lebanon.

And then one evening I walked out onto the terrace and knew the rain was coming. I could smell it in the air. I climbed up onto the roof and watched as light clouds began to move in from the north. Slowly the dust dissolved, the air cooled and freshened, and people's foreheads cleared as they lifted their heads to the hint of moisture.

The next morning, I was awakened by what sounded like someone dropping marbles one by one onto the flagstone terrace. Half-awake and puzzled, I went out. It was rain. Just a few heavy drops at first, coming down one by one, hitting the bone-dry ground and bouncing off it as though they were solid. Then more came down, and more, and within five minutes they were beating on the ground with the rhythm of a tabla player, the rapid heavy beat of the Middle East. Only the first rain is ever so loud.

Birds woke out of their torpor and joined in like flutes to the drumbeat. Thunder rolled over the hills, adding in bass. Huge black clouds moved over the landscape, sweeping in one after the other as the wind picked up. Sheets of rain slashed across the valley like huge white curtains, and suddenly the whole of Gehenna was in flood. The dry wadi had become a torrent of water. It ran off the rocky hillsides, spilled down over the terraced walls, and came cascading through the valley for all the world as though Gehenna were a natural river, speeding on down into the drought of the desert.

In town, cars skidded on the oily combination of dust and water. Housewives rushed for the laundry hanging out to dry. Small boys set up instant umbrella stalls on Jaffa Road. Pedestrians waded through the streams of water running down the hilly streets and leaped over huge puddles as the drains gargled and choked at the sudden onslaught. Gutters gave way under the weight of water. Dry branches fell from the trees. Tile roofs in the older neighborhoods leaked where nesting birds had nudged aside a tile or two in the spring. Rahamim Cohen took his phone off the hook; he was one of the last expert roofers left in the city, and he couldn't work in any case until everything was dry again.

An hour later, it was over. Only the smell remained. The smell of damp earth, of bushes and trees coming back to life with water, of wet clothes and soggy sandals and drying hair. The smell of freshness.

Miri came around. Tall, lithe, with long blond hair darkened by the rain. Born to Ilana the day before the '67 war, she was seventeen now. Soon she'd be going into the army. Her sandals and jeans and faded cotton shirt were soaked. She hung them to dry in the bathroom, I gave her some dry clothes and a spare pair of sneakers, and we drove off for the Jericho road to look for flash floods in the desert.

For both of us, the desert was part of our landscape, part of our personal map of Jerusalem. It seemed natural enough to just get in the car and go. Once it would have been. But now as we crossed the former Green Line from Israel proper into occupied territory, I felt a certain uneasiness. And that was new to me.

✡

Israel has held the territories now for longer than not. For nineteen years, from 1948 to 1967, it was a tiny country. Unless you owned a large world map, the name of Israel wouldn't even fit over its territory and was written instead in the middle of the eastern Mediterranean, with a line pointing toward the Israeli coast. Its shape was convoluted by the ceasefire lines of 1949, a challenge to any child trying to draw its outline in geography class.

The '67 war solved the problem for the schoolchildren. Suddenly there was the clean straight line of the Jordan Valley instead of the complex kidney shape of the West Bank pushing into Israel. At first, there was another line too: the Green Line. This was the name given the pre-1967 borders of Israel.

I don't know why the line was called green. I do know that there have been other green lines in this century in similar situations. Perhaps the military mapmakers have a limited supply of colors. Red would be too provocative; blue and black already exist; yellow would not show up well. So green it was. I also know that Israelis explained the color to each other through the old pioneering idea that Israel would make the land bloom. "Look," they would say as they crossed the line to tour the West Bank after the war, "you can see where the border was: on one side it's green, on the other it's brown." This was true in places where there was a border kibbutz or a forest, but for the most part that green was in the mind's eye. The West Bank is no greener today for all the Israeli settlements there than it was in 1967.

In any case, the Green Line did not last long. Like all her generation and all those born after her, Miri had only the vaguest idea of where it was. How was she to know? You can't find a map with the pre-1967 border on it anymore, not unless you happen on one at the back of a long-unopened drawer or in an archive or an outdated textbook. An Israeli aged thirty today — a schoolchild in 1967 — has no memory of a small, brave little Israel. It seems natural that Israel should be the size it is, West Bank and all. The idea of giving it back has faded in the minds of younger Israelis along with the memory that it was taken in the first place.

Miri at least knew what the Green Line meant. Just the week before, she had come home in great excitement. She was to spend her army service in Nahal, the wing of the military that sets up new kibbutzim in underpopulated areas and on the border. She would be one of the founders of a new kibbutz. And the main income of that kibbutz would come from growing flowers.

David and Ilana laughed in pleasure. They had also started out their adult lives on a kibbutz. And growing flowers was a wonderful way to do army service. "Where will it be?" asked David.

"Near Jericho. But don't worry, it's inside the Green Line."

The trouble was that if it was anywhere within a twenty-five-mile radius of Jericho, it was beyond the line. "Oh, no," said Miri, "I know it's far closer than that."

There was a flurry of phone calls, and finally clarification: the new kibbutz would be near Hebron, not Jericho, and it would indeed be just inside the Green Line. Everybody in the house relaxed. In most Israeli households, it wouldn't even have been an issue; only the minority still questions the right of Israeli settlement beyond the Green Line.

Now as we drove on down the Jericho road, Miri was far more aware of the whole issue than she had been a week before. She talked about an item in that morning's paper. In Israel's main security jail in the Negev, one of the first terrorists from the West Bank, sentenced to life in late 1967 for planting a bomb in a West Jerusalem building, had just met his seventeen-year-old brother. The two had never laid eyes on each other before. The younger brother had just been given a five-year sentence for throwing stones at Israeli cars driving through the West Bank. I had noticed the article too. The two photographs had stared up from the page, side by side. The older brother had narrowed eyes and a broken nose, and that taut, gaunt look of someone used to being in jail. The younger, the same age as Miri, still had the softness of childhood. I remembered wondering how long it would be until the younger brother began to look like the elder. "That older brother has been in jail almost as long as I've lived," said Miri, her forehead creasing as she tried to imagine having spent her whole life behind bars.

✡

To a stranger, the West Bank doesn't look as though it's worth serving life for. Much of it is in the rain shadow of the Jerusalem mountains, harsh desert hills falling way down beneath sea level to the stifling heat of the Jordan Valley and the sulfurous air of the Dead Sea. The unenchanted eye sees only dun color in every direction. The hills are naked, the bones of the earth deprived of fleshy trees and shrubs, stripped bare of all pretense to civilization. The northern part is gentler, foreshadowing the green of the Galilee, but the hills are still undeniably made of stone, and to eke a living out of them is backbreaking work.

Yet there is enchantment hidden in this harshness. You can fall in love with this landscape. Israeli environmentalists have. Unlike environmentalists elsewhere, who tend to be liberal, they are about evenly split between doves and hawks — those who want to keep and annex this land, and those who are willing to give it back for peace.

The hawks make the West Bank their own by hiking through it, often with Bible in hand. Each spot mentioned in the Bible is further proof that this land is their destiny, and that it is theirs by an ancient right far stronger than present-day realities.

And the doves? Without the Bible and without the politics, the truth is that we also have made it ours. We were pulled to the magic of deep wadis containing hidden pools of water. We sought shade beneath the walls of desert monasteries or in the long-abandoned hermits' caves nearby. We soaked under the waterfall in Wadi Qelt. We fell with cries and huge splashes into the rock pools of Wadi Darja. We watched with awe as a flash flood filled a familiar dry wadi with a raging torrent of rock and water, and the occasional goat or sheep was swept off its feet to its death. In those first years after the '67 war, we wandered through the *shuk* of Hebron, wondering what was in the greened parchment boxes piled high around the walls of the apothecary stalls. We bought myrrh and frankincense there, and gorged ourselves on sticky flat cakes of honey and goat cheese.

By the time Gush Emunim had built Kiryat Arba, the fortresslike Jewish township dominating the hill overlooking Arab Hebron, the knifings in the *shuk* had begun, and the shootings and beatings in reprisal. But by then we were used to the convenience of the West Bank. It now took two hours to drive to the Galilee through Jericho, instead of three and a half as before. An hour and a quarter to Beersheba via Hebron, instead of two and a half. We no longer had to drive the long way around. We could go direct, through the picturesque villages and winding roads of occupied territory.

For a year in the late seventies, I drove the Hebron road

south from Jerusalem quite regularly. I spent most of that year in the Negev and the Sinai, coming up to the city every couple of weeks to touch base. In summer I'd drive at night because it was cooler then. I'd sing at the top of my voice as I drove, the windows down and the warm air curling around the back of my neck. Sometimes I'd see foxes and wolves in the headlights. Other times I'd drive early in the day, watching the rising sun bring range after range of hills into early-morning focus, glancing as the glassmakers near Hebron stoked up their furnaces for the day's work.

"But shouldn't you carry a gun?" people said. "How can you drive that road alone? It's not safe." Yet I felt no sense of threat. And the very idea of carrying a gun alarmed me. What if someone stole it? What would I do if I ever pointed it at someone? Shoot?

But there were many other Israelis, the settlers, who did carry guns, and who did take them out and shoot as the younger generation of the occupied began to raise the level of resistance, blocking the road with burning tires and throwing stones. Some of the shots wounded, some killed. Among the dead was an eight-year-old girl.

When you first hear of it, throwing stones can seem a relatively harmless form of protest. But stones can be as dangerous as bullets. A friend driving from Jerusalem to Beersheba one morning found that out. He was hit in the head by a stone. His skull was cut open, and his brains glistened in the sunlight. He crashed the car, managed to crawl out of it, and then watched in horror as a mob of stone-throwing children began to advance on him. A military jeep arrived just in time.

He was a dove (and still is), but how were they to know that? So far as they were concerned, he was the occupier, clearly identifiable by the license plates on his car.

Most of this violence began after I had left, as the Begin regime strengthened the Jewish settlers' movement and threatened annexation. And then the odd murders began, like those of the two hikers at Cremisan. Single incidents here and there, but enough to raise the level of fear.

Some Israelis began to drive the long way around again. Others checked out what was happening first, avoiding certain times: when high school students finished classes, or when men were coming out of the mosques. They began to travel at night or in the early morning, or on Shabbat, when the settlers, nearly all religious, do not drive and it is clear that any Israeli on the roads is not one of them. If there were news reports of "disturbances" on the West Bank, they adjusted their plans accordingly.

The "disturbances" could be due to any of the many anniversaries marked in the West Bank. The day of Israel's conquest of Jerusalem, for instance, or the day the peace treaty with Egypt was signed, or the day a child was killed by settlers on the Hebron road. Few Israelis drive through the West Bank then. Those who still do so travel together in a caravan of two or three cars, or they take a gun, or both. To be an occupier is to live in fear of those whose lands you occupy. And the more the Begin government insisted that the West Bank was an integral part of Israel, the less Israelis felt comfortable there.

With each visit back after I had left, I began to see that it was no longer too wise to take off into the desert alone as I had once done. I used to laugh at those who thought I should carry a gun. Now I resented them. Violence had increased on the West Bank. Gush Emunim settlers and Kahane's thugs marched through the Hebron *shuk* with fingers on the triggers of their submachine guns, heads pushed forward on their necks in search of trouble. Terror begat terror in biblical escalation, until the gun toters won the day. Their need to rule by force had forced me and others like me into fear.

Only when I had to think twice about going into the West Bank did I realize how used to it I had become. I had taken it for granted as part of the space of living in Jerusalem. I would miss it if it were no longer open to me, and resent it if I had to present a passport at the border.

"Perhaps it was only a dream," as one of modern Israel's first poets, Rachel Blaustein, wrote about the early idealistic days of pioneer settlement. But dreams die hard. Perhaps it was only a dream that I ever wandered around freely, without fear, in occupied territory, as a welcome guest and not as an occupier. Perhaps that was only how I saw myself. After all, that freedom of movement was protected by an army. I had chosen to ignore that. It had been a false freedom. I was never a welcome guest, and that is now clear.

There is no longer room for illusion. That in itself may be for the best, but it makes life far more difficult. As Gush Emunim vigilantism and then outright terror grew, I was forced to see myself through Palestinian eyes — as much the occupier as the most violent psychopath among Kahane's "boys." In this part of the world there is no standing aside. You become forced into roles that violence determines for you, no matter how much you oppose them. And that is the real loss of freedom, far more painful than any limitation on freedom of movement.

✡

All that said, Miri and I managed to ignore it for a brief couple of hours that day of the first rain. We were too excited by the idea of seeing flash floods. Our hopes were high. A swift river of water ran parallel to the road, where there was usually a dry gully. Rocks and foam bounced on its surface. Deeper into the desert, it would be even more dramatic.

But by the time we climbed down into one of the long, deep ravines that cuts through the desert, there was only a small stream left at the bottom. We were too late; the flood had already been. Bedouin goats were clambering up the steep mountainside opposite, their feet unusually clumsy under the weight of their round, water-distended bellies.

We set off back the long way around, on side roads. And suddenly, still in the desert, we were driving through a new city suburb. Four-story buildings were packed together in the usual fortress formation on the crest of a hill, ugly and silly in their geometric rectitude. Nobody was living there yet, but it looked almost ready for occupation. A sign proclaimed it to be Pisgat Ze'ev. I was amazed. On my last visit, only a year before, this had still been at the talking stage. Now it was stark reality, a new Jewish suburb of Jerusalem reaching far out into the desert.

To approach Jerusalem from the east was always special. You drove for hours through the desert, and then up the sharp incline from the Dead Sea. Then at a certain rise in the road, you saw three spires pointing into the sky on the high horizon: the church on the Mount of Olives, the tower of the Augusta Victoria hospital, and the tower of the Hebrew University on Mount Scopus. They were signs high in the air as you drove on upward, beckoning you, promises of Jerusalem unseen just the other side of that mountain ridge.

Now new fortress suburbs guard the eastern entrance to the city. Maaleh Adumim sprawls over hill after hill to the southeast, and Pisgat Ze'ev to the northeast, both dominating the landscape and ignoring the older wisdom of Arab villages built into the sides of the hills, blending with them.

Workers were putting the final touches to Pisgat Ze'ev: retaining walls for gardens, pavements, windows and doors. They shouted greetings as we drove by. They were all Arab. As usual, only the contractors would be Jewish. It is a peculiar irony that every new Jewish suburb and settlement around Jerusalem and in the West Bank has been built by Arab labor. The old days of pride in Jewish labor are alive only in the kibbutzim. Miri told me the joke about an old socialist pioneer taking his grandson for a walk in Tel Aviv. "You see that building there?" he said, pointing with pride. "I worked as a bricklayer on that building." The child stared at him in surprise. "Why, Grandpa," he said, "I didn't know you used to be an Arab."

Like most of the jokes told in Israel nowadays, it was too close to the bone to be funny.

We came out of Pisgat Ze'ev near the Arab suburb of Beit Hanina, on the Jerusalem-Ramallah road. I had visited here often in the late sixties, during the sudden burst of friendship between Arabs and Jews that followed the '67 war. Those days, it seemed that we could solve the whole conflict just by being friends. If we could do all the things that are the normal content of friendship — talk, eat, drink, play pool — we could overcome politics. But there was no normality to it. The rush to friendship had something of "Me Tarzan, you Jane" about it. We wanted to know each other, but not simply as people. Arab wanted to know Jew, and Jew, Arab. But the fact that one was a Jew and the other an Arab was not enough. Too many of those friendships were based, not on personalities, but on the sole common interest that we had been enemies. Not surprisingly, few of them lasted. And as the political situation worsened, it became clear that while good acquaintances might still be possible, real friendships were not. A Green Line of the mind took the place of the missing line on the map.

Miri listened open-mouthed as I talked about that time, responding to her questions. It seemed another age to her. She had been a toddler then. "Do you think it's still possible?" she asked. "Peace, I mean."

"I don't know," I replied. "I do know that we have to believe it's possible, because the moment we stop believing that, we close the circle. We have to keep hoping and trying and believing. Otherwise, if we give up, we resign ourselves to violence."

She nodded reflectively. "I had a dream the other night," she said. The dream had disturbed her, showing her a part of herself she hadn't known existed. In it, she had been standing on a balcony in Haifa with a friend, looking out at the view. A group of Arabs and Jews came out together onto the balcony of a nearby house. There was food and drink, and everyone seemed to be enjoying themselves. Somebody brought out flutes and drums, and some played while others danced. "See," Miri said to her friend, "Arabs and Jews can be friends." But even as she spoke, the music changed. It became wild and frightening, and as the two watched in horror, the flutes turned to guns in the hands of the Arabs and they began firing at the Jews, killing them all.

There was nothing for me to say. There is no comfort to be had in this country. It is a place that makes you have dreams you do not want, and that makes you acknowledge things in yourself you would rather not know. The sun shone palely through the last of the clouds as we drove past the Old City on the way home, but it was late afternoon and there was little warmth in it.

VI

Once, Jerusalem was the center of the world. An ancient map shows it that way. The city is the heart of a huge three-petaled flower, and the petals are marked Africa, Asia and Europe. The map was made in the sixteenth century, when people still mapped what they felt rather than what they measured.

One sign that it may be time to leave Jerusalem is when you find yourself thinking that perhaps that ancient mapmaker was right. Everyone seems to pass through the city sooner or later, until you begin to feel that if you just sit here long enough, the world will come to you.

When it does, the world is at its best. Easy to forget that a visiting writer or actor is sailing on the results of hard work done in the past. You see the final results, the polished forms, not the work that went into them. You see the face of success without the sweat. These visitors, whom you may have read about in *Time* or *Newsweek,* will tell you wonderful, witty stories of life in the cultural center, be it New York or London or Paris. And that life seems all the more glittering and sophisticated for being filtered through the presence and words of its stars.

Jerusalem attracts them in a way that Tel Aviv cannot. Because Jerusalem too has that star quality — a name that reverberates in people's minds throughout the world. A name that is bigger than the place itself. This makes it both provincial and cosmopolitan, a city of paradox: neglected and desired, small and large, personal and political, immediate and ancient.

But to live here and really love the place, you need an appreciation of the provincial. Of the inevitable chance encounter. Of life circling back on itself. Or of the fact that the real center of the world is a floor crowded with green baize tables under ancient domed ceilings, where the sound of clicking balls rises up through small windows set into the domes and on out over the Old City roofs. It is a pool hall, right at the point where the Moslem, Christian and Jewish quarters of the Old City meet. And that is its name: the Center of the World.

The name seems entirely appropriate. The very idea of a pool hall being the center of the world has an element of studiedly careless fortuitousness, which is the best way to exist in this city. And it provides a good balance to the naive seriousness of the medieval mapmaker. It keeps things in proportion.

That is especially important in a city where people tend to lose proportion.

The provincial asserts itself again on Ben-Yehuda Street, the main commercial stretch of West Jerusalem. The street has been converted into a café-lined pedestrian mall, but many of the old-time stores have survived — tiny drab emporia of buttons and lace, dowdy clothes and cheap metal souvenirs. The chic new stores don't open up here anymore; they are in the Cardo in the Old City, where the tourists are. The only tourists in Ben-Yehuda Street are the last of the hippies, picking up the odd shekel by strumming a guitar and then lying on the warm paving stones to rest as the Israeli world passes them by.

Friday mornings, it seems as though half the town is here. Backslapping youths elbow their way through the crowd, loud-voiced and cheerful. Screams of "Yossi!" or "Shoshi!" cut through the throng as those crowded around the rickety plastic café tables try for the attention of friends walking by. People carry string bags, lick at dripping Popsicles, munch on felafel in pita. The men have paunches, even those under thirty. The women's faces seem haggard. The Israeli aversion to deodorant is all too apparent. Here and there a well-dressed young woman stands out from the rest. Eyes follow her down the street, taking in cut and color, admiring yet resentful at the same time. "She must be from Tel Aviv," someone says.

A small group huddles around a palm reader. A religious youth with guitar yells out the repetitive words to "Am Yisrael Hai," "The People of Israel Lives," which has become the theme song of the ultranationalist right wing. His head is thrown back and his eyes rolled up as though these three words could transport him to the other Jerusalem, the heavenly one. At the other end of the street, a ragged messianic preacher stands with flute in hand. Drums, a Jew's harp and big crudely drawn posters are spread on the ground around him. He's off on a free-association rap about the messiah and music and rebuilding the temple and great days in the making, slipping from one thought to another in one long unintelligible sentence. People have gathered around him. They're drinking in the monotonous chant of words, mesmerizing in its madness. Jerusalem may not have changed so much after all in two or three thousand years. Then too there were instant prophets and mad seers blinded by their faith to the existence of others, chanting and drumming and strumming themselves into ecstasy.

Large and small, heavenly and earthly, always blending. But the blades of the blender are blunted, and the mix churns uneasily, ready to explode, to burst off the lid and run wild. Jerusalem does not have the grace of knowing that it is provincial. For most Jerusalemites, the city still *is* the center of the world.

They talk proudly of the fact that this country hosts the largest foreign press corps in the world after Washington. Or that coverage of Israel in the American press equals coverage of the Soviet Union (a judgment, I would have thought, more on the quality of American coverage of the Soviets than on the importance of Israel). Our political conflict gives us the illusion of importance. It keeps us in the forefront of world attention.

I think it was Mussolini who once said that he welcomed more enemies, because the more he had, the greater his status. And sometimes I wonder if we are not caught in that same self-defeating bind. So long as we remain in conflict, we remain interesting — to the world, and even worse, to ourselves.

The fact is that the wars bind us. Perverse, but true. We measure time by wars. "I did this before the '73 war." "That happened just after the '67 war." "They got married during the Lebanon war." One of Yehuda Amichai's poems touches the heart of it: "Even my loves are measured by wars . . ." And such measures are more than points on a calendar. They are measures of mood, and measures of experience. We understand each other by which wars we have lived through. They create a bond of adversity as strong as bonds of love.

The continual up and down of politics binds us too. For me it would begin every day at six in the morning, when I went down to the corner store for milk and the papers. If the deliveries were late, I'd listen to the early news broadcast with Shimon, the store owner, and we'd get into a discussion — usually calm enough, but sometimes heated. The milkman occasionally joined in when he arrived. The newspaper man never did. He had enough of the news in delivering it.

This is a place where everything seems to end up in the news, down to who called whom what at that morning's cabinet meeting (a crescendo of epithets when Arik Sharon gets going, from "liar" and "insane" to "criminal" and "traitor"). A place that suffers six scandals a week (and none on the seventh day, when no newspapers are published). A place where ordinary people face moral dilemmas that others elsewhere never imagine: whether to do army service in Lebanon or the West Bank or to refuse and risk jail, or even whether to stay or to leave.

Such a place operates continually on the high thin ridge of excitement between life and death. In "Thoughts for the Time on War and Death," Freud wrote that "life loses interest when the highest stake in the game, life itself, may not be risked." The first time I read that, I was shocked. But that was before I came to Israel. Here, that stake lends everything that happens an intensity and sharpness of experience that makes life elsewhere seem dull by comparison.

We become hooked on it. Junkies of passion. Sometimes we sit and dream of the quiet life — New Zealand perhaps, or the standard Greek-island fantasy. But we know that after a few weeks we would start whittling and gnawing at the edges of it, pacing up and down in frustration at contentment. Once you get used to that constant high level of excitement, it works like a drug. It doesn't matter whether it's good or bad, painful or happy. It can be war, especially when that war is short and sharp. It can be peace, as in the exultant high of the Sadat visit to Jerusalem in 1977. It can be love or it can be loss. But the terrible truth is that if you stay in Israel over a certain amount of time, everything "normal" becomes pointless and even decadent, like sex with someone you don't really care about — nice enough as long as it lasts, but a hollow, empty feeling afterward.

The constant picking at meaning and motive is both exhilarating and exhausting. We live on an emotional roller coaster. And we are addicted to the ride.

✡

We were eight people that evening — six friends and a visiting writer and his wife — lingering over the dinner table. At first, it looked as though we would achieve the minor miracle of escaping political talk. There must have been something with ginger in the dessert, because we talked about *taglach*. I rhapsodized about the ones my grandmother used to make: big hard balls of dough with a giant raisin in the middle, dipped in crystallized ginger, a child's delight of sharp, tooth-breaking sweetness. Hers were Latvian, but the *real* taglach, argued Arele, a political scientist, were the Polish ones, which are runny with a hole in the middle.

He told a story that was probably apocryphal, since some of us had heard it before. A friend visiting South Africa was asked by someone there to take a batch of taglach to a mutual friend in Tel Aviv. No problem, of course. But on a stopover in London, he realized that the gingered honey had seeped through its packaging and into his clothes in the suitcase. Annoyed, he threw the taglach into the wastebasket in his hotel room. When he got home, he saw the mutual friend and told him what had happened, expecting laughter and apologies. Instead, the man went white: inside the taglach had been diamonds.

Politics eased closer as Dalya made the coffee. Yoske, an expert on Arab affairs, was not long back from reserve army service in Lebanon. He was one of the few Israelis who appreciated the complexities and subtleties of the internecine situation there, and had suffered continual frustration as his superiors refused to listen to his warnings that they were alienating the Shiites. Now he entertained us by telling the story of his role as a mediator in a conflict between Shiites and Phalangists over a jeep.

As we sat contentedly, nursing the coffee, the story began to wind in and out, backward and forward, building into arabesques of Byzantine complexity. Soon there were as many dramatis personae as in a Gabriel García Márquez novel. Multiple layers of honor and pride, tradition and machismo obscured the simple original motive of greed for a jeep. It couldn't even be established whose jeep it had been in the first place. And in the end, of course, the jeep was burned.

Inevitably, conversation now turned to an analysis of the latest events in Lebanon. Odd, I thought, how three years before we all knew next to nothing about that country. War is a terrifyingly direct way of learning.

Dalya and I began a quiet tête-à-tête as the others discussed the logistics of a possible Israeli withdrawal. "Have you really left?" she asked solicitously, as though asking if it were true that I was seriously ill.

I shook my head in confusion. "Yes, I've left, but being here. . . . It makes it hard to accept. You know, you make a decision, and then you find it's tougher to carry out than you thought. It should be simple enough, God knows, but . . . ." I shrugged instead of finishing the sentence.

"Do you think you'll come back?" she asked tentatively.

I'd been asked that question many times since I'd arrived. Practice had formed an answer. "I don't know," I said. "Not yet, in any case." The first time that answer had slipped out, it had surprised me. I hadn't thought about coming back. But it had felt right, so I stuck with it. It smoothed the sharp edges of leaving.

Dalya smiled. It was a small, sad smile, but it eased the lines from her face and reminded me how beautiful she could still look. "It's odd, you know. I know I tried to persuade you not to leave. I still thought then that everyone should come here, to this country. But in the last few years . . ." It was her turn to shake her head in confusion. "I seem now to be on the left, when I always thought of myself as being in the center. And in fact, I don't think I've changed. It's just that the center has swung to the right. And I can't encourage anyone to come here anymore. For the first time I can sympathize with those who leave. I can see the sense in it. I wouldn't dare tell you not to leave now."

"So why do *you* stay? Yoske still has an American passport. You could leave easily enough."

"Because there's so much to be done here," she replied, unconvincingly. And then, convincingly, "And because the children are here." Her younger son was just going into the army, her older son into university. "But if Arik Sharon ever becomes prime minister, then I swear I'll leave."

Many people I knew had said that in the seventies about Menachem Begin. Yet they had stayed and suffered through the seven years of Beginite madness. And they were still suffering in Lebanon from the results of that hysterical grandiosity with its technicolor dreams of history writ large. "I doubt if you'd leave even then," I said. "People don't leave for political reasons."

"No, but for all the reasons that politics affects. We were in London for a few months last year, when Yoske was doing research. And it was so relaxing. *Not* knowing everything that was happening. *Not* talking politics, because it was considered rude. Not endlessly discussing, not being constantly involved. We went to theater and movies, and we had amusing irrelevant conversations with people we met. It was like living a normal life. It was wonderful.''

"That's what I thought about New York at first,'' I said, "but then after a while the normality of it became too much. You begin to realize that few people really care. Here, political passion comes with the territory. There, it's suspect. Everything can pass there because most people are too busy with the details of their own private lives. And that's alienating. You're right: it's wonderful to just stand apart for a while, just be a spectator. But I wonder if we're really even capable of that anymore. After all, could you have stayed in London?''

We both sighed. The sighs were long and deep and familiar. And then a small quiet question slipped out of me. "What if there were peace? What if things were as we would like them to be? If there were full peace, if we were to come to terms with the Arab countries, with the Palestinians, with the Israeli Arabs, everybody? What if we solved it all? What then?''

She gave me an odd quizzical look, then sat back and stared a moment into the distance, as though seeing another country. And then she gave a rueful smile. "You know,'' she said, "I think of what life must be like in a small town in New Zealand . . .''

✡

New Zealand claims a special place in the Middle Eastern heart. It is another country of the mind. A green country. A peaceful country.

"It's not like here,'' says the cabdriver hero of Yitzhak Ben-

Ner's novella *A Far-off Country*. He is obsessed by New Zealand and collects anything to do with it: travel brochures, coins, stamps, press clippings, postcards, buttons from AN-ZAC uniforms. . . . His life's dream is to take his whole family to live there. Then everything will be fine, all problems resolved. They'll have a farm, his kids will shape up, his nerves will calm down.

His nemesis is a beautiful young blond woman with blue eyes whom he picks up one day as a fare. She comes from New Zealand. He becomes obsessed with her too, and talks endlessly to her in his mind. "In 1967 they proved in a world survey, with computers and all, that New Zealand is the only country in the world that is completely stable and peaceful," he imagines telling her. "There it's a dream. It's a paradise. A place where when seventeen sheep are killed by a train it makes the headlines, big black letters right across the top of the front page."

This is the Israeli fantasy: a place where sheep are killed, not people. Where the ram is sacrificed instead of Isaac. Again and again, New Zealand sneaks into Israeli conversations, usually at the stage where that deep sigh is heaved. Then quietly, wistfully, after a short silence: "I wonder what it would be like to just pick up and go to New Zealand," or "Maybe we should all just go to New Zealand," or "You know, Shaked went to New Zealand . . ."

But Shaked came back from New Zealand after a year. Nobody knows anyone who went there and stayed. In fact Shaked might be the only one who went there at all. New Zealand is the fantasy, and as such, it must remain separate from reality — a refuge of the mind.

And not only the Israeli mind. Perhaps in Poland too they speak wistfully of New Zealand. And in El Salvador. And Northern Ireland. I know they do in Egypt.

I found that out early in 1980, less than a year after the peace treaty had been signed. I was on assignment for an American magazine, and the Cairenes had opened both hearts and homes to me. They were intrigued perhaps by this combination of Israeli and Britisher and by the idea of a journalist in search of conversation rather than that day's headlines.

Salah Jahine and I first met in the lobby of my hotel, where he had come to pick me up. "How will I know you?" I'd asked over the phone. "I am fat," came the answer in a slow mordant voice.

I'd laughed and made the usual crack about a copy of the *Financial Times* under his arm. But when I got down to the lobby I saw immediately that Salah didn't need that. He was indeed fat — a dark, fully rounded Hitchcock figure.

That first meeting was the only time I ever saw him in western dress. At home or in a restaurant, he wore a galabiya, which made him seem even larger than he was but far more comfortable. He was a man of many talents, as Cairenes often are: political cartoonist for *Al Ahram,* the country's leading paper; actor and television personality; poet; lyricist for Egypt's national anthem; satirical lyricist; Egyptian representative to the World Peace Council; children's theater puppeteer. We talked often, in long rambling conversations that wound in and out of politics, books and personal histories. As he talked, he'd fondle his giant poodle — one of the outward signs, as my presence might also have been, of his distaste for the strictures of fundamentalist Islam, which sees both dogs and unveiled women as sources of contamination.

In his study, a black stone head of Ptolemy rested sideways on a cushion in the bookshelf. When I asked why he didn't have it mounted, he turned a mournful eye to it and murmured: "It's there to remind me of what we do, we Egyptians, sleeping on the pillow of history."

Sometimes it seemed that we tore that pillow apart, scattering feathers as we traced the cycles of enmity and grandiosity down from the old-time pharaohs to the modern ones — Sadat and Begin, the peacemakers, both entranced by the grand sweep of history. But you can only trace such things so far until you fall into silence. When we did, Salah finally heaved a tremendous sigh. It reached deep down inside him, making his whole body tremble, shaking his many chins, and frightening away the dog. "Ah well," he said, "there's always New Zealand."

He looked at me reproachfully as I began to laugh. "I'm sorry," I said as the laughter subsided. "It's just that your sigh is so familiar — from Israel." It was oddly disquieting to come to what had been enemy country and find the same dream of peace and quiet cherished by people on the other side of the border.

Nearly five years later, as Dalya and I sighed in Jerusalem, I wondered if there was a New Zealand twin to this fresh green image deep in the heart of the Middle East. What did New Zealanders see when they thought of Jerusalem? A celestial city glowing in shimmering lights, perhaps, or the romanticized excitement of war, or the grave importance of international relations. . . .

"They probably don't think of it at all," said Dalya. "They probably don't have to. They're probably content with what they have."

"Probably," I murmured. Yet I wondered if it were really so.

Dalya's image of peace as life in a small town in New Zealand had implied a place of boredom and provinciality. Not a place she would choose to be. Only much later in the evening, after I'd left, did I realize how strange that was. She could have been a political hawk talking, not a dove.

VII

THE next morning I went running. I took what had become my regular route: down into Gehenna, past the Cinemateque, along the gravel path beneath the cliffs, and then on down the rough track that leads to the village of Silwan and the perennial spring that is the only reason Jerusalem ever came into being five millennia ago.

But Gehenna is not the reservoir track in Central Park. My foot caught in a rut, my ankle twisted, and I limped back to Mishkenot. Gehenna was still dangerous after all.

The ankle healed in a few days, and then my knee suddenly gave way with agonizing pain. "There's a loose ligament there," said the doctor. A kind smiling face, a gentle touch, silver hair: a gentleman from prewar Europe. Hard to imagine there was any knee problem he hadn't seen. "The ligament can't hold the kneecap properly, so it keeps slipping out of place, and that's when you feel the pain."

"You mean it dislocates?"

"That's right," he said, and sent me off to a physiotherapist who sentenced me to lift weights.

That evening, I lay on the worn Persian carpet in Ilana's living room and lifted apples tied to my ankles in plastic bags. I was comfortable in this house. I had spent a lot of time here over the years, and now there were bits of me scattered through it: an old rolltop desk, an ornately carved wall clock with a uniquely quirky sense of time, and various prints, pictures and books, all left with Ilana and David when I'd sold my house.

The television news was on, and Ilana and I listened and talked at the same time. The program began, as usual, with the latest report from what the press now called "the quagmire of Lebanon." It was clear by now that it was by far the worst of Israel's wars. Begin and Sharon had meant it to be a lightning strike, a '67 kind of war that would conveniently annihilate the PLO. Somehow, the two men clung to that image as those summer weeks of 1982 dragged by. As Israeli tanks broke down and whole columns came under fire, immobilized. As casualties mounted and the air force was sent in to bomb Beirut. As West Beirut was placed under siege, with water and electricity cut off for days at a time at the height of the summer heat. As rats played on trash piles and flies swarmed and rubble filled the streets. As journalists drank in the bar of the Commodore Hotel and socialites sunbathed on the Corniche and families crouched in terror in their hallways. As Phalangists slaughtered Palestinians and Israeli soldiers stood by, watching them go in, listening, and doing nothing. And even then it wouldn't finish. Soon, soldiers would bitterly call it "the thousand-day war."

The soldiers in this news report could have been on the Purple Heart Trail in Vietnam. They were patrolling the Litani River, picking their way through the high reeds, heads swiveling on tense necks, eyes bulging with the effort to see what might or might not be there. There were casualties nearly every day now — mines, booby traps, sudden assaults. As the reporter asked questions, the soldiers searched for words they never thought they'd need — words that could express the sense of being strangers in a strange land, unwanted and hated, without any sense of rightness in what they were doing.

"Home," they kept saying. "All we want is to go home. Tell them that at home. Tell the government. We want home."

I envied them their knowledge of where home was. The apples hung heavy from my ankles. "I feel so foolish," I said, raising my laden legs one by one as a political analyst came on the screen to comment. "Here I am trying to leave this place, trying to walk on out of here, and I go and dislocate my knee." The apples were getting heavier all the time. "How am I meant to find my place in this world when I can't even keep my knee in the right place?"

The dog came over and licked my face in commiseration. Ilana looked over archly from the sofa, the gray streaks in her hair gleaming in the lamplight. "Perhaps it's a matter of relocation, not dislocation."

I sat up sharply. "That can't be," I said miserably. "I'm meant to be leaving."

The funeral of the six hundred and third Israeli soldier killed in Lebanon was on the screen now. He was forty. He had come to Israel at age five — from Lebanon.

"What can I tell you?" said Ilana. She was used to these funerals by now. "You know what's happening, yet here you are, split between Jerusalem and New York. You'll decide very soon. There's a limit to how long you can go on with a divided heart."

Maybe that was where the ligament was loose. In my heart.

I lay back and went on lifting my legs, thinking back to our phone call early on in the Lebanon war. Deracinated Israelis had been calling each other frantically in New York: "What's happening? Did you call home? What did they say?"

We had called home, making sure that those we loved were still alive. Once it was our friends we worried about. Now it was our friends' children. And all of us with that unspoken question: What about their children in turn? Would we be calling to make sure they were all right in another twenty years, in yet another war?

"Bo'az is fine," Ilana had said the moment she heard my voice on the wire. "He's commanding a tank, but he's fine." She talked about that tank for a while. At one point it had been covered with flowers as Christian Lebanese villagers welcomed the Israeli invasion. There was even an armored-corps order not to throw soda bottles out of tanks so as not to pollute the environment.

"But . . . whole streets in Tyre and Sidon are in rubble from bombardment," I said.

"What do you mean? How do you know?"

"We see it here in the States every night on the news."

There was a silence. Just the units ticking by on the international line. "They're not showing any of that here," she said finally, her voice flat and tight.

We went on talking, but I felt strange, distant and stupid. My voice echoed back to me on the transatlantic cable, my own words haunting me as I spoke: "Should I come back? I feel so useless here!"

"How do you think *we* feel?"

"But at least there you're all in it together. Here . . . This is the first war I've been outside the country, and I know it sounds odd, but it's worse than being there. People here ask me what's happening, but it hurts too much to explain, so I evade the questions and then they're insulted, as though I'm trying to hide something from them. And I suppose they're right, I am. I'm hiding the pain."

"You sound lonely," said Ilana. In Jerusalem you can never be lonely in wartime. "Well, that's exile for you."

The word hit me like a blow to the stomach. I sat in shocked silence. Ilana took a deep breath. "Listen, you have to face the simple fact of it: you can't be in two places at once. You've left. If you want to come back, then *tfaddal,* do that. But you can't go on sitting there in New York and thinking about being in Jerusalem. That way, you'll end up neither place.''

That had been more than two years before, and the war was still going on. The funeral report on the television news was coming to an end. The words of the commander at the graveside rang hollow. The dead soldier had been a good man, a good comrade in arms, a good husband, a good son; sometimes it seemed as though they were burying the same person night after night. There were the friends from the unit with tight lips and muscles twitching in their cheeks, the wife held up by women relatives either side of her, the mother hiding her face beneath a shawl. At least in military funerals they used coffins. There wasn't that sickening thud of a shrouded body hitting the ground. They used coffins for good reason. This soldier's jeep had been blown up, and there was no knowing how much of him they'd been able to pick up afterward.

Ilana got up quickly and went to make some coffee. ''You see what you've missed by being in New York? This is our nightly entertainment now — Arik's war. In Lebanon they call Sharon the butcher of Beirut. But what about this country? How many more Israelis are going to have to die before we realize that he's butchering this country too?''

✡

The start of that war was the end of all innocence for us. I remember Yaron's place in New York in early July 1982. Sun shining through the townhouse windows, sounds of Spanish filtering through the ferns as children played in the street, comfortable sofas in the book-lined study: it was the Israeli dream of the good life. The Israel Defense Forces were stalled at the edge of Beirut.

Yaron was sitting uncomfortably on the edge of a sofa, a tall figure bent in defeat, his gray curly hair falling over the deep furrows of his forehead. He had been a Palmach commander in 1948. Now his son by his first marriage was a paratroop commander in Lebanon — "in a foreign country," he said bitterly. "And the more I think about it, the more this Israel of Sharon and Begin is a foreign country for me." He looked up a moment, gray eyes staring at me with the chill clarity of despair. "We're all exiles in any case, so what difference does it make where we're in exile? There's internal exile in Israel, or physical exile in New York." His head drooped again, and his hands hung loose over his knees. "Perhaps it's easier in physical exile," he whispered.

A month later he was on the plane, unable to stay away. Three months later so was I. But what did we come back to on those visits, exiles of choice like Yaron and I? Coming back was hope and fear, memory and nostalgia. It was the awful tension between what once was, what could have been, what is, and what might yet be.

"We're all exiles in any case," Yaron had said. Yes, all with multiple tales of exile. I am the daughter of exiles who themselves were children of exiles. From Latvia through Ireland to England, three generations, each born in a different country. And then my own journeying, from England to Israel to the United States. Had I now doubled that history of exile, becoming a double exile myself? Had I taken up what Czeslaw Milosz calls "the vocation of exile," in which homelessness becomes a permanent state of mind and you belong to neither the country you left nor the country you came to?

I had gone to Israel, the country that prides itself above all on being a homeland. A home for the Jews. Return. You can come home again. A strange word, *homeland,* as though a whole country can be home. No wonder it carries disappointment and disillusionment for many. A whole country cannot be home; it becomes home only when you find your place in it. And then I had left this second home for the foreign land of New York, where the homeless wander the streets and inside the condos and the co-ops, behind the plants and the Japanese paper blinds, few people are native New Yorkers.

It seems a strange irony now that the only plant that ever grew well in my house in Israel was the creeping philodendron known as "the wandering Jew." It is the country's favorite indoor plant, the easiest to care for and the hardest to kill by neglect.

Sometimes I wonder if I have incorporated the legend of the wandering Jew — if I am somehow fated never to find simple content, never to settle down in the simple assurance that this is my place, where I belong. I don't know how many people ever consciously do that. Perhaps most people don't even ask such questions. But Jews do. We have all incorporated that legend to some extent, even though it is not ours.

Two thousand years ago, the story goes, a Jewish cobbler had a store on Jerusalem's Via Dolorosa. The Friday of the Crucifixion, he watched along with everyone else as Jesus dragged the cross up the long street to Calvary. It was his misfortune, perhaps, that Jesus asked to rest against his storefront. The cobbler refused, and for that Jesus condemned him to eternal wandering, with never a place to rest.

Somehow I never quite realized that the legend was not Jewish but Christian, and had served for centuries as a focus for antisemitism. Then a few years ago, I came across a beautifully bound volume called *The Legend of the Wander-*

ing Jew on the shelves of a used-book store in California. It was clearly the author's lifework — a long, rambling compilation of every reference to the legend in folklore, songs, archives and literature from the sixth century to the twentieth. The book was expensive, and the style was very academic; I was about to put it back on the shelf when I noticed the title of Appendix B: "The Legend of the Wandering Jewess." It was one and a half pages long. I laughed, and bought the book.

That evening, at dinner with friends, I told them about my find, and chanted the refrain of a twelfth-century English folksong that had already imprinted itself on my memory: "Repent repent O England, repent while thou hast space / And do not like the wicked Jews deny God's proffered grace."

There was an uncomfortable silence around the table. Faces were blank with surprise where I had expected laughter. And then I realized that I was the only Jew at the table. You do have to be Jewish after all. I had thought the jingle funny, and in repeating it had expressed the black humor of the in-group — in the wrong circumstance. That too was part of being in exile.

When you have too many worlds, you begin to confuse them. People like me are supposed to be cosmopolitan. Able to live in and adjust to different societies, we are often envied for our chameleonlike adaptiveness, our breadth of reference and our range of association. We are considered well educated, well traveled, knowledgeable, adept: citizens of the world. Except that when you are a citizen of the world, you are a citizen of no place in particular.

I should be better at it. After all, Jews are surely the emigrants par excellence. The original emigrants of western civilization, in fact. Out of Egypt, out of Babylon, out of Israel . . . We *know* about emigration. A restless people, they say. The State of Israel was meant to put a stop to the wandering, but it didn't. It just added another layer of irony to it. Now the same number of Israelis live abroad as live in Jerusalem.

A line of philosopher-novelist John Berger's has stayed with me: "To emigrate is always to dismantle the center of the world, and so to move into a lost, disoriented world of fragments." It is to tear apart that flower with Jerusalem at its center, plucking the petals one by one until the center withers and dies.

And I didn't want it to die.

VIII

THE Godly ice cream van was parked at a crazy angle by the windmill at the top of Yemin Moshe. That's how I had thought of it since the first time I'd seen it, from a distance, and missed the single dot in the Hebrew lettering that changed the company name from Godly to Goodly. It must once have been shocking pink, but the shock had long faded under the combined assault of sun, dust and neglect. Its fenders were bent, its chrome rusted, and the driver's window was cracked. One of the tires was flat. There was nobody in it, though tourists making an early start were already gathering nearby, following the advice of guidebooks touting the spot as one of the best vantage points in the city.

An American couple in their fifties were standing by the van, map in hand. "Are you from here?" they asked as I passed by. I nodded. "Can you tell us where is Mount Zion?"

I smiled with the pride of ownership. "Here's Mount Zion," I said with an expansive sweep of my arm. "Right here."

They peered over the narrow valley, faces creased in disbelief. "That?" they said incredulously. "Are you sure?"

I left them looking up and down from map to view, trying to put together the Mount Zion of their imagination — rising majestically tall from a flat plain, the way children draw mountains — with this gentle hill before them, just another of Jerusalem's many hills. This one was particularly pretty, to be sure, but it was clearly not what they wanted. It was not their idea of what Mount Zion should be.

I felt sorry for them as I went on down the steps. I would hate to be confronted with that disparity between the image and the reality. I would hate to be a tourist here, stuck with the surface of things and cut off from the people and the passions, lovemaking and stone throwing, quiet hope and noisy despair that make the city.

Pale people stare hassle-eyed into the street from the coffee houses of the Old City. They have the weary resigned look of most tourists here. It is a test of faith for them. In their minds is a holy city; around them is a Middle Eastern city geared up for tourism.

Once there were grocery stores, ironmongers, and storefronts with undefined businesses, where hookah-smoking old men passed the day playing backgammon. But they are fast disappearing from the Old City streets. The Bedouin have sold off all their old embroidery and jewelry years ago, and neckpieces from Bedouin dresses that I once gave as presents are now worth small fortunes. On the Via Dolorosa, the Baudawin Shop still sells good antiquities — at bad prices — and the nuns still sit in their little storefront, painting icons. But otherwise, you are assaulted by the most extraordinary collection of kitsch: plastic rosaries and worry beads; crudely carved olivewood camels and crucifixes; scarab necklaces imported from Cairo at twenty for a dollar and sold here for twenty dollars apiece; pants made from the worn skirts of old Bedouin dresses; copper trays and coffeepots that may later turn out to be tin; cheap cotton skirts and shirts from India and Taiwan; badly painted ''Armenian'' pottery made in Hebron; overly bright ''Hebron'' glass blown in Jerusalem;

ceramic tiles painted with slogans such as Shalom Y'All; Coca-Cola tee shirts in Hebrew or Arabic; fake inlaid mother-of-pearl boxes; horsewhips bound with plastic masquerading as leather; beads and bangles made of glass and plastic and tin; synthetic "sheepskin" rugs; polyester galabiyas and keffiyas. And herded together in the midst of it all, flocks of tourists, their tour guides waving little flags on poles so that lost sheep can find them in the crush. They block the narrow alleys, solid walls of bewildered humanity that give way only when sack-laden donkeys stumble into them, goaded on by young boys screaming warnings and curses in Arabic.

It is cleaner now than it used to be. You have to go deep into the markets to find the stalls with sheep's heads drooping bloodily outside, and even the flies buzzing around the dead eyes seem to have been decimated. The streets are paved with new flagstones — an expensive municipal project after the old streets had been torn up and the whole sewage system of the Old City revamped (causing considerable paranoia among the Arab residents, who may indeed have had plenty of reason to be paranoid, but certainly not this one).

Outside the Holy Sepulchre, where the Emperor Constantine's mother insisted she had found the remains of the True Cross, an Israeli tour guide explains to his Evangelical group that what the Moslems call the Mosque of Omar on the Temple Mount is not the real one, since the real one is right here beside the Holy Sepulchre. Nobody looks interested. He doesn't say much about the Sepulchre itself before taking the group inside; he just tells a joke (a few desultory laughs) and waves his hand at yet another Station of the Cross up a flight of steps beside the entrance. Nobody pays any attention to the Crusader crosses etched into the stone walls and pillars by pilgrims centuries ago; tiny and exact, they are carved one right next to the other in row upon row, as though some prisoner of faith had been incarcerated here and had counted off each day by making a cross instead of an *X*.

What do modern-day pilgrims make of it all? The Roman Catholics know what they're doing when they make their pilgrimage to Rome, not to Jerusalem. Rome has a European respect for the appearances of religion. Here, in the Middle East, the eastern churches reign supreme, and religion is earthly and earthy. Prostitutes used to ply their trade inside the Church of the Holy Sepulchre in the Middle Ages. There's an old legend that children conceived there will be children of good fortune. Belief in it may still be alive: in 1970, a couple were arrested *in flagrante delicto* on the main altar. If I remember correctly, he was Moslem and she Christian.

✡

People looking for one Jerusalem and finding another strive to reconcile the two in their minds. Better, perhaps, never to come here — to stay where belief can exist pure and unsullied by experience, where the heavenly Jerusalem floats alone in the clouds without any ties to the earthly one. When you live in a city like this, it is easy to forget what it means for those who have never been here. I was sharply reminded of that some years ago, where I least expected it: in Ireland.

I had been driving slowly through the mountains of the south, taking the long way around to a rendezvous a few days later in Galway. I was lost, and pleased at it. There was the simple pleasure of freewheeling down mountainsides, watching deer and rabbits spring up in surprise as I went by. Or of stopping here and there to drink from a stream and take in this vast amount of greenness, stunning to someone used to the desert colors of the Middle East.

Toward late afternoon, it occurred to me that I should find my way back to a road large enough to be on the map. I came down a mountainside and saw help: a small stream rushing over rocks, sheep grazing on the banks of the stream, a small humpbacked stone bridge, and leaning on the parapet of the bridge, a man — the shepherd. I pulled up nearby, got out, and walked up to him.

He said good day to me, and I to him, and I realized that I had interrupted his reading. I leaned over and looked at the book. It was the Bible. We talked for a few minutes of sheep and deer and the weather, and of my being lost. He introduced himself. "Michael," he said, "after the archangel." I told him my name. "And where would you be coming from?" he asked. From Dublin, I said. "Ah yes, but you wouldn't be Irish, not with that voice on you. Where would you be living?"

"Jerusalem."

He gave me a strange sideways look, squinted in suspicion, and suddenly became very abrupt. "Well then," he said, drawing himself upright, "you'll be wanting this road. . . ." He gave me the directions and turned back to his Bible without even saying good-bye.

I wasn't sure what to make of it. Perhaps he was an antisemite? Or perhaps he'd just had enough of talking. Whichever, there was clearly no more talking to be done with him, so I went back to the car, followed his directions, which were correct, and continued on my way.

I solved the puzzle a week later, back in Dublin. It was a rainy afternoon, perfect weather for the old covered markets known as the Liberties. I spent a good part of it sipping tea and negotiating the price of an old concordance with a talkative Irishwoman who had lots of time on her hands. When she asked where I lived, I told her Jerusalem. And she too gave me that strange sideways look. Only she made the meaning of it quite clear:

"Now who d'you think you'd be fooling with an answer like that? Sure you haven't the looks of someone who'd be living in Jerusalem."

"Why not?" I asked, puzzled by her reaction.

"But Jerusalem's a holy city, to be sure. A city for holy people, my girl, not for the likes of you and me."

And suddenly I saw the Jerusalem in her mind — a city of spires and bells and chants of praise, high above the clouds, bathed in light, where only holy people could live. "People like her don't live in Jerusalem," that shepherd down south must have thought. "Does she think she can be pulling my leg because she sees I'm reading the Holy Book?"

Yet the bells and the spires and the chants of praise do exist. Not in the clouds and not in heaven, but very much on earth. Jerusalem still lives off its holiness, as it always has. And every April, secular Jerusalemites flee to Eilat or to the Galilee or even to Tel Aviv as hordes, herds, swarms and throngs of pilgrims choke the streets: Jews for Passover, Christians for Easter.

Faith can still be innocent. On the roof of the Holy Sepulchre, the Ethiopians celebrate Easter with drums and silver rattles, chanting slowly and mournfully with eyes raised as the slow cadence enters the soul. A tent has been set up, lined with leopardskin-printed cotton. Inside, beautiful women with dark, dark skin and finely chiseled features sit in flowing white robes, smiling and talking softly. It could be a scene from a Delacroix painting, to be called "The Court of the Queen of Sheba," perhaps. The men too are beautiful, dressed in leggings and long tunics and sari-like shawls made from the same flowing white cotton as the women's dresses. The children are miniatures of their parents — "little chocolate angels," says a friend. Their eyes shine with quiet excitement at being up so late, here on the roof, with the air mild and the stars bright overhead and the insistent rhythm of the drums beating out of the chapel.

But below them, in the main basilica, there are no children. The Russian and Greek Orthodox worshippers crowd around the main altar, shoving and elbowing each other for an advantageous view. The air is thick with incense, so thick that it stings the eyes. The primary color here is the black of the nuns' robes. They have been here since the night before, coming in early to stake out floor space for the Miracle of the Holy Fire — a very reliable miracle, occurring at one o'clock every Easter Saturday. Fire sprouts up of its own volition inside the square housing of the main altar, reaches out through a hole in the side, and lights the candles of those closest to it, who in turn light the candles of those behind them. Candle lights candle so quickly that within half a minute the whole church seems alive with flame. It is clear enough that the priests light a torch inside the altar and hand it out through the hole, and it is hard to believe that this whole mass of people has absolute faith in the miracle. But their faces say they do.

Now the Russian nuns shine with their own inner fire as they hold their candles above their breasts, each candle with its own little doily around the stem to prevent hot wax dripping onto fervent fingers. These are peasant faces, smooth and ruddy-cheeked, full of a vicious naïveté that could stone you to death as easily as worship you.

As midnight nears, the main bell goes into a dirge. It rings once, heavily. The reverberations take a full minute to die. Then it rings again, another single time. And then again. And again. The sound is terrifying. In the courtyard outside, groups of young men and women hang around spitting sunflower seeds, chewing gum and smoking, waiting for something to happen just as their counterparts must have done two thousand years ago in this same place. Inside, mouths bend eagerly to the Stone of the Unction, kissing, licking and wiping the holy water from the stone where holy flesh was once washed. The eye picks up the gaudy finery of crosses and chalices and the torn raiment of the acolytes. The smell of mothballs from the priests' robes penetrates the cover of incense. But none of this makes any difference to the hordes of little Greek ladies, bent with age, who sit on their camp stools and wait for resurrection, crossing themselves again and again to keep faith alive.

And all the time, just a couple of hundred yards away, black-robed Jews with long sidelocks bend and sway at the Wailing Wall, wrapping the leather thongs of their phylacteries around their arms and heads, binding themselves into their faith. As the church bell peals out its dirge, they chant all the louder, resentful of others worshipping a different god so close by. Waiting for the messiah, they may also envy those whose messiah has already come.

Secular Israelis have taken to calling them "black Jews" because of their dress: the black coats, black leggings and wide black hats have been incongruously transplanted from the icy gray landscape of the old eastern European shtetls, chilling the eye even in this land of sun and stone. These men of black now threaten to take over the whole city as they have already taken over the Wall.

✡

Once, the Wall was everybody's. At least it was for a short time, after '67, when the popular photograph was taken of the young paratrooper, helmet in hand and face grimy with battle, weeping by the huge ashlar stones. I saw the Wall for the first time not long after that photograph was taken. It was Shavuot, the feast of the first fruits and one of Judaism's three festivals of pilgrimage to Jerusalem. That day, I felt like a pilgrim.

It was a perfect Jerusalem summer's day, warm and dry. In the couple of weeks since East Jerusalem had been conquered, the authorities had been working overtime. Never before had Israeli contractors worked so quickly. Mandelbaum Gate, the corrugated-iron-roofed checkpoint between East and West Jerusalem, had been torn down. A new road had been paved from the Municipality, near the border, on down the side of the Old City to Damascus Gate. The Wailing Wall had been renamed the Western Wall; there was no more cause for tears, it was said. And hundreds of houses built in front of the Wall over the past few centuries had been torn down, leaving a huge dusty lot. It was to that lot that tens of thousands of us made a pilgrimage that day. The rest of the Old City was still closed to civilians.

Most of us came because it was our first chance to enter forbidden territory. We wanted to see, not to pray. We joined the line at the top of Mount Zion, armed with fruit and nuts and canteens of water. As we came over the crest of the mountain, crossing the border, we saw the long line of people winding slowly down through pines and olive trees to the low arch of Dung Gate and then into the Old City itself.

It was a peaceful line. Nobody pushed or shoved. Bare-armed socialists rubbed shoulders with black-garbed Hassids, believers with nonbelievers. The barriers were down. And as we shuffled slowly on down the mountainside, dust gathered on our feet, working its way into our pores and covering our sandals until by the time we reached the gate we had true pilgrims' feet, pale with dust — feet that looked as though they had walked many miles and many days to reach this goal.

Ilana held Miri in her arms. Bo'az tagged along beside David, hanging on to his hand with a five-year-old's trust and singing to himself. People who knew each other in the line went backward or forward to say hello, smiling and crying, often at the same time. Ilana and I wore big floppy straw hats. It wasn't a holy day; it was a holiday.

Inside the gate, the dust clung still thicker to our feet. We didn't ask then what had happened to the people whose houses had been pulled down. We were too excited, part of the mass of people pressing on toward the Wall. And then there it was, and there was that first feeling of disappointment at how small it seemed until you were pressed right up against it, and there was the claustrophobia of the crush, and the amazement at so much emotion over stones.

They were big stones, certainly: beautifully worked ashlars, some of them sixteen feet by three. But still, they were stones, impassive to the excitement they created. The turtledoves living in the upper reaches looked down in avian superiority, peering through the caper bushes that grew out of the cracks between the stones. I was grateful for the birds and the capers. They made the stones human somehow. In fact, they made me laugh.

There was no wailing, not then. Six years later, after another war, I would go down to the Wall again with Ilana. That was the Yom Kippur War. We had just heard of a close friend's death at the Suez Canal. And I would watch with horror and respect as Ilana touched those smooth stones, polished by millions of heads and hands and fingertips over the centuries, and began to wail. The sound was primordial, animal-like, terrifying — a sound that would break the hearts of angels, if they had hearts to be broken.

Some say they do. The Wall has many legends, as any wall of tears must. One has it that this wall survived the Roman destruction of the Second Temple due to the tears of the archangel Gabriel. When he saw the temple in flames he flew down to earth, sat on the western part of the temple's retaining wall, and wept. Where his tears fell, the stone hardened and refused to crumble. (I liked that story when I first heard it — until I realized that nearly the whole of that Herodian retaining wall is still there, eastern, western, northern and southern. You have to ignore a lot to believe in legends.)

And even though archangels may have hearts, stones don't. Worshippers write prayers and pleas and hopes on little pieces of paper and push them between the stones, but they never reach heaven as they are meant to. Instead, the rabbis of the Wall take them out and bury them. I never dared take one out to read, having the respect of the secular for the belief of the faithful, but others have. They found prayers for health and pleas for blessings and success in love or work or school — bland, prosaic messages to God, all requests and no thanks. I was disappointed, though I'm not sure just what I expected.

I never prayed at the Wall, but we have our own history, that wall and I. Many years ago, I wandered down there late one night, after a party on the roof of the once-splendid Petra Hotel inside Jaffa Gate. The Petra was the stoned hippie center of the late sixties. The party would go on dutifully until dawn but I was not really in the mood for it, preferring the solitary sound of my footsteps echoing in the stone alleys and tunnels of the Old City until a flight of steps spilled me out into the huge plaza in front of the Wall.

It had been partitioned by then. Everything here gets partitioned sooner or later. In the case of the Wall, it was sooner — right after that first Shavuot, in fact. Two-thirds had been sectioned off for men, one-third for women. Couples could no longer stand in front of it with their infants in their arms, as Ilana and David had done. Lovers were separated. The rabbis of the Wall were on round-the-clock watch, ensuring that men's heads and women's arms and legs were covered, handing out dowdy pieces of gray shawling at the entrance to the women's section, black yarmulkes on the men's side. There was no gaiety here anymore. This was serious business, these stones holy stuff.

I am inclined to believe the story about the two hippies who came into the tunnel beside the men's section one day dressed in galabiyas. They were long-haired and long-bearded, and their eyes shone with LSD. After some whispered discussion among the guardians of the Wall, the two were approached and asked to explain their presence. "I'm Moses," said the one, "and this is my brother Aaron." The rabbi turned to his confreres, eyes wide in disbelief, and muttered: "But it can't be — Moses died before he could see the Land of Israel. . . ."

That night of the Petra party, the rabbi on duty was asleep. There was nobody else around. I paused at the high fence separating the men's and women's sections, and then walked down into the men's. I looked up, but saw no movement. Doves, like rabbis, need their sleep.

The Wall was higher now than it had been. Aware that it seemed peculiarly low after the plaza had been cleared, the rabbis had dug down an extra three ashlars in depth. Here and there, a piece of paper poked out from between the stones. I stared, wondering what those with faith saw here.

Strange, I thought, that a people so opposed to idolatry should make a shrine of a wall. And not even the wall of the temple itself, but just part of the retaining wall of the Temple Mount. But then perhaps idolatry is a basic human need, like shelter and security and love and warmth. Or perhaps it's what people seek out when shelter and security and love and warmth are threatened. It becomes the physical equivalent of the strong leader that people yearn for in hard times.

"A stiff-necked people." I can't remember who first called the Jews that. Probably one of the prophets. But it seems appropriate that such a people should choose to worship at a wall, knocking their heads against stone. And ironic that the wall they chose has for centuries supported a different temple of a different people — the Islamic shrines of the El-Aqsa mosque and the Dome of the Rock. Temple rights clash under the Judean sun.

I breathed in deep and smelled the warmth of that sun radiating off the stones into the cool night air. The damp pre-dawn breeze was just starting, making Jerusalemites stir in their sleep and pull up the covers. I stretched out my hands and touched the Wall. I felt . . . stone. I shrugged. This wasn't the place for me. I turned to leave.

Then somewhere above me, something moved. I heard a rustle followed by a grating sound, looked up, and quickly moved aside. A stone glanced off my right shoulder and fell with a loud clatter to the ground. I reached for the shoulder as a sharp pain spread through it. A small shower of dust floated down over me. All was silent again.

I stepped back to see. Although the crescent moon gave a little light, I could see no movement up there. There was a bit of blood on my shoulder, but no real damage. I bent down to pick up the stone; it was a rough piece, the span of my hand, and weighed a couple of pounds. Lucky I'd moved in time. It must have fallen from the rough-worked upper section of the Wall, but why on me? And what had moved it? A dove stirring in its sleep, perhaps, or the breeze, or time. . . . "Damn wall," I thought. "Another few inches and it could have knocked me out."

I weighed the stone a bit longer in my hand, then dropped it. There was an argument now between this wall and me. A very personal argument. "Damn wall," I muttered again, but there was just the mountain silence in answer. I turned and began the walk home.

It was only years later that I thought it odd I hadn't taken that stone with me. But then who would have believed me? It looked like any other piece of stone in Jerusalem. And besides, by then I wanted nothing to do with stones and religion.

IX

THE stone walls of Mea She'arim are drab and gray. I rarely go there, since this ultra-Orthodox neighborhood is a mini-state unto itself. When I do go, I feel as though I should have presented a passport at the border, or as though I have walked through a time warp into an eighteenth-century eastern European shtetl.

The narrow streets are crowded with black-garbed men sporting long sidelocks and wide fur hats. Women keep close to the walls, dressed in clothes two sizes too large for them lest their figures show and tempt the men. The children are animated by the look of fervent righteousness in their eyes. Everyone has the pale skin of an indoors life. Signs admonish "the daughters of Israel" to dress modestly, and young girls wear thick lisle stockings even in the height of summer. Other signs threaten the bell, book and candle of excommunication for such sins as owning a television set.

Stories of Mea She'arim life once ran like wildfire through the rest of Jerusalem: couples had intercourse on Friday nights through a hole in the sheet between them; ritualized orgies took place as a certain sect carried on the forbidden practices of a seventeenth-century false messiah; certain rabbis claimed *droit du seigneur* with a bride, preceding the husband in the wedding bed. Because the ultra-Orthodox were so obsessed with hiding sex, the stories about them invariably focused on the sexual. And of course there was no way to prove that they were false.

We laughed at that obsession with hiddenness, yet we were fascinated by it too. For the most part, we maintained an attitude of superior tolerance, though that tolerance was strained every now and again by what were called incidents.

One of the worst involved Dan. As though he hadn't been injured enough in real wars, he had to take the blows of this one too. It had been in the mid-sixties, when he was recovering from a bad traffic accident. Though he was back to work, he was still on crutches. An urgent story came up on Shabbat, and like any conscientious journalist, he rushed to the scene. Without thinking, he drove the quickest way, which was through Mea She'arim. He never got that story. A crowd of rock-throwing youths stopped his car, screaming "Shabbes! Shabbes!" in outrage at this flagrant violation of the sanctity of the Sabbath day. They dragged him from the car, broke his crutches, and beat him mercilessly until one woman living nearby, retaining something of the spirit of Judaism instead of the letter of the Judaic law, decided that to make a phone call to the police on Shabbat might be allowable if it would save a life.

Dan had to stay on the crutches a few months longer than he had expected, and since that time, police barriers have been set up every Shabbat all around Mea She'arim, sealing it off to traffic and to the world.

Things might have stayed like that were it not for the Six Days War. The fruits of victory drew the ultra-Orthodox out of their Mea She'arim stronghold, and they took over the Wall. And as they began to flex their muscles in the real world of Israel, secular tolerance for them began to wane. It is hard to tolerate intolerance.

They became very good with stones. Stoning, after all, is the biblical punishment par excellence. They stoned policemen trying to break up their demonstrations against autopsies, and they stoned cars traveling on Shabbat to the new suburb of Ramot. They stoned archeologists who they claimed were "desecrating ancient Jewish graves," and they even stoned buses serving their own streets because the bus company had displayed sexy swimsuit ads on bus shelters elsewhere in the city. There were injuries from these stonings, but because the vagaries of domestic politics had given the ultra-Orthodox political parties disproportionate power, the stoners were not even arrested, let alone tried. A Palestinian boy stoning cars in the West Bank was sentenced to five years, but these "zealots," as the press politely called them, were protected.

Their language of hate was archaic, a throwback to times we had thought long past. "Infidels," they screamed at us as the stones flew. "Sadducees, Roman quislings, lovers of Hellenic culture. . . . Intermarrying, swine-eating, Sabbath-breaking heretics. . . . Tramplers on the graves of the forefathers." Secular humanists were a pale shadow of what we became in their eyes.

Their violence increased with their political power under the successive Begin governments. Secular Israelis hoped for a new sanity when Shimon Peres became prime minister in 1984, but he seemed powerless to stop them. Diners were beaten up in restaurants serving bread on Passover. Meat stores selling nonkosher meat were vandalized. Car tires were slashed and secular children threatened in neighborhoods close to ultra-Orthodox ones until families sold their homes and moved. Soon there was talk of a Bible Belt stretching across the whole of north Jerusalem. And in other parts of the city, a pattern seemed to be developing: first one ultra-Orthodox family moved in, then another and another, and then a yeshiva opened up, and then they began pressuring for certain streets to be closed on Shabbat. . . .

The sex life of Mea She'arim interested nobody anymore. The latest rumor around town was that the ultra-Orthodox were moving into secular neighborhoods on purpose: it was all part of a campaign orchestrated and financed from New York so that they could gain control over the whole city. It was hard to decide if the rumor was paranoid or sensible.

Secular Jerusalemites began thinking about what had once been the unthinkable: moving to Tel Aviv. The popular Jerusalem paper *Kol Ha'Ir* started a regular column profiling those who had "emigrated" to Tel Aviv, as well as Tel Avivians who had "immigrated" to Jerusalem. Oded, still writing his column despite his doubts, came back from a couple of days in Tel Aviv entranced by the idea that you could buy flowers on Dizengoff Street at one in the morning. "It's sane down there," he said. "It's normal. It's a regular city, with beautiful women in the streets and people in cafés and clubs late at night, laughing and joking, all with endless things to talk about besides politics and religion."

The difference between the two cities was brought home most sharply when "zealots" decided to demonstrate — violently — against Shabbat-morning seminars in the Habimah Theater. The mayor of Tel Aviv refused to capitulate to their demands or to tolerate such behavior. "Tel Aviv will not be a second Jerusalem," he said. Secular Jerusalemites drew the conclusion: our city was already lost.

The bitterness of that thought infected us all. To our horror, we began to return intolerance for intolerance.

After lunch with Dan one day I was driving him home, negotiating the narrow streets near the center of town. A "black Jew" was walking in the middle of the street. He moved out of the way only at the last moment, with what seemed deliberate slowness. I sped by. "Damn," I joked, "missed again. I thought I'd run him over."

Dan laughed uncomfortably, perhaps remembering that beating of twenty years before. "That's what I sometimes think too," he said. "But what's happening to *us,* that we have fantasies of running them over?"

"They want to run us out, we want to run them over." I shrugged. "The difference is that we know we'll never do it — and they know they will."

"Not so long as Teddy's still mayor," said Dan.

Teddy Kollek — no self-respecting Jerusalemite calls him anything except Teddy — has been mayor of Jerusalem since 1965. He's been reelected each time as an independent, the vote for him an anomaly in a city that generally votes more to the right than the rest of the country. A sturdy, bulky man, he has one of the toughest jobs in the world. And one of the most seductive.

I have never dreamed of being prime minister, or president, or defense minister. But the mayor of Jerusalem — that is the stuff of legend. Even the stuff of poems. "It's sad / To be the Mayor of Jerusalem. / It is terrible. / How could any man be the mayor of a city like that?" wrote Yehuda Amichai. Hard to imagine a poem about the mayor of New York.

Amichai is right. It is a terrible job. Somehow, Teddy has managed, over twenty years, to keep all the elements of this city in some kind of balance. Jerusalem is one of the most deeply divided cities in the world, yet at least the division has remained, for the most part, workable. It can be lived with.

What had been a cultural backwater became a center under Teddy's administration. He raised the funds for the Israel Museum, beautified the city through the Jerusalem Foundation, developed the Israel Festival and the biennial Jerusalem

Book Fair, encouraged the Jerusalem Film Festival, and tirelessly brought cultural figures here, getting them involved with the city. He maneuvered among the multitude of political pressures, giving in where he had to. Sometimes he made bad mistakes. The worst was the most visible — the fortress style of the new suburbs built since 1967 to ring the city with Jewish housing — though a mere mayor could have little effect on what was essentially political architecture. In general, however, he walked the tightrope of his job with a degree of influence and determination available only to a man this stubborn, politically adept and, when he wanted to be, charming. We criticized Teddy, certainly, but at each election we voted for him again, aware that Teddy was what stood between us and our fears.

"Think what Jerusalem would have been like since 1967 without him," said Dan. That was a nightmare. And for avoiding that nightmare, there was now a committee to nominate Teddy for the Nobel Peace Prize.

The trouble was that Teddy was now in his seventies. How much longer could he keep on, and who would come after him? We looked at the array of forces on the city council and saw the future: a combination of ultranationalist and religious forces strong enough to put in whomever they chose unless Teddy was there to run against them.

Jerusalem without Teddy? I had visions of a benighted city inhabited by religious fanatics; of riots and violence and more blood in those ancient blood-soaked alleys as the tension between Arabs and Jews strained the limits of coexistence. Teddy had somehow managed to keep the peace — or at least an uneasy truce — in the battle between the religious and the secular for the soul of the city.

But now that battle has spread to the whole country. It has become the major undertone to Israeli life. "The question is whose country it will be — theirs or ours," said Dan. Like him, I had never been antireligious before. But as the battle lines were drawn, I could feel anger and resentment growing in me, as though I were being pushed to the wall. How much longer could we last until the vision of another poet came into being, the poet whose lines were deeply etched into the images of our fears:

> *Things fall apart; the center cannot hold;*
> *Mere anarchy is loosed upon the world,*
> *The blood-dimmed tide is loosed, and everywhere*
> *The ceremony of innocence is drowned.*

Yeats called that poem "The Second Coming."

✡

Meshiach achshav, "Messiah Now," said the bumper sticker on the white Peugeot in front of me as I drove by the King David Hotel. I did a double take. It was in the same print as the Peace Now stickers, and the same colors. From a distance, the two could have been the same. I stared so hard that I didn't notice the car's brake lights as it slowed for a pedestrian crossing, and almost crashed into the back of it.

The driver didn't look as though he were expecting the messiah to walk out in front of him. His small knitted yarmulke, neatly trimmed beard and plaid open-necked shirt proclaimed him to be one of the "modern Orthodox," religious but not a Mea She'arim zealot. A zealot of another kind instead. The bumper sticker indicated that he was from Gush Emunim, "The Bloc of the Faithful" — the ultra-right-wing messianist movement that had spearheaded Jewish settlement throughout the West Bank in the belief that once this was achieved, the messiah would come. It was Gush Emunim's job to help him on his way.

For myself, I didn't mind at all if the messiah were to come, or whether it was for the first or the second time. I considered that none of my affair. It became my affair, however, when certain people decided he needed an assist — especially since I did not want to be around when their messiah came. This messiah inspired his followers to intimidate West Bank residents, to confiscate their land, to beat them up in their homes and shoot them in the streets and blow them up in their cars. He was the messiah of thuggery and terrorism.

The "black Jews" consider it sinful to do anything to help the messiah on his way, because that would be usurping the power of God. (Some of them therefore oppose the Jewish state as an unjustified human striving for something only heavenly power could bring about.) But these Gush Emunim religious Jews have no such qualms. They combine yeshiva studies with army service, and are considered fully integrated into Israeli society. Many think the direct text of the Bible more important than the refinements of ethics and values argued out over centuries in the Talmud. The Talmud is of and for the Diaspora, they say; leave that to the ultra-Orthodox. The Bible holds the revealed words of a higher force, and that is of and for the Land of Israel.

The Bible makes for strange bedfellows. A fundamentalist devotion to its written word is the cement for the unholy alliance between the Moral Majority in the United States and Gush Emunim in the West Bank. This involved Christian moneys being sent to the Jewish terrorist underground, and unwavering support of the Israeli government in its most expansionist Beginist phase. The reason for the alliance is simple enough: both groups are expecting the messiah. A different messiah, to be sure, but then each group expects the other to be surprised when the time comes.

I first came across the Christian fundamentalist scenario in an abandoned mining town in Nevada. The population was fourteen, and one of those fourteen lived in a house made entirely out of old Budweiser bottles. Chickens scratched for pieces of straw in the dust of the front yard; in the backyard, a dish antenna brought Oral Roberts and other preachers across the desert. The television sat incongruously in one of the two rooms, both of them laid out as a museum of mining life. Old spoons, soap boxes, pans, coat buttons, news sheets, knives, guns, tin cups, medicine bottles, shoes, sieves, packs and whiskey flasks were displayed on the shelves. On the way out, there was a rack of small cartoon booklets. PLEASE TAKE ONE, said the hand-lettered sign on top. My eye caught a yellow Star of David on the cover of one booklet. It was called "Support Your Local Jew." I flipped through it, gasped in astonishment, and took all six copies that were on the rack. I couldn't imagine where the local Jew might be in these parts.

The point of the booklet was quite clear: if you didn't support your local Jew, you were asking for trouble. Egypt was once a great civilization, but it didn't support its local Jews, and now look at the place. Rome and Babylon and Persia made the same mistake; these Jews can make empires crumble. Germany didn't support its local Jew (a rather cute way of putting it), and now half of its population lived under Communism as a result. England's empire disintegrated because it never followed through on the Balfour Declaration promise of a homeland in Palestine. And now Russia would be destroyed for also not supporting its local Jew. How that would happen was all foretold in the Bible. First there'd be World War III, which would kill off a quarter of the world's population. Then seven years of further strife in which two-thirds of the world's Jews would die. And then, finally, Armageddon. But when all seems lost, Israel's messiah will "burst through the clouds and save her." (A drawing here of a chariot racing down from the clouds, with rays of light all around it.) And then, "Israel gets her greatest shock." (We see a drawing of a hand with a stain in the middle of the palm.) "Her messiah will have nail prints in His hands." He will be Jesus come the second time. At that point, all surviving Jews will accept Jesus, and what remains of the world will be saved.

Armageddon in Nevada made a certain sense. The brimstone of nearby Death Valley was far closer to this primitive vision than to the real thing — Har Megiddo, the gentle hill in the lower Galilee whose name was corrupted to render the English Armageddon. You can go up it the easy way, by road, or else race straight up through the woods to the top, scratched, tired and proud, as Israeli grade-schoolers do every year on class outings. For Israelis, Har Megiddo is not an idea; it's a real place.

But fundamentalism denies reality. The myth is all that counts; the real thing is irrelevant. As are people. Easy to talk about mass death — one-quarter of the world's population, two-thirds of the world's Jews — when you have depersonalized people.

What struck me most about "Support Your Local Jew" was the peculiar mix of support and fear, amity and hate of Jews. This mix seemed to run all through the Christian fundamentalist movement, which showed clear signs of antisemitism. The head of the Moral Majority office in New York had marveled at "the Jews' God-given talent for making money." The head of a large southern Baptist church had proclaimed that God did not hear the prayers of Jews. Yet the whole movement admired and supported an expansionist Israel, so much so that Menachem Begin awarded a medal to Jerry Falwell, the head of the Moral Majority, for his services to Israel.

The two fundamentalist groups, Christian and Jewish, were bound by a direct interest in disaster. The greater the disaster, the closer we would come to Armageddon, and the closer to that, the closer to the messiah. But while the Christian role was one of moral and occasional financial support, the Jewish fundamentalists were hell-bent on bringing about that disaster.

I spent some time with Gush Emunim activists in various settlements around the West Bank in 1978, researching a long article on what was happening there. It could be that they were so convinced of the justice and inevitability of their cause that it made no difference what they told me; it could be that they felt safe talking, knowing the degree of their support in the government; it could simply be that they didn't care what they told me since they knew I could do nothing about it. But whatever the reason, they talked.

They told me that they were stockpiling arms. That the Dome of the Rock and the El-Aqsa mosque were a blight on the Temple Mount and would have to be destroyed. That if the Israeli government would not drive the Arabs out of the West Bank, they would do the job themselves. Israeli law was irrelevant, they said. The "normal law" of others did not apply to them. They had a higher mission, indeed a "higher law," dictated to them in the Bible. "We have the power to bring about the messiah," they told me, eyes burning with belief.

A vengeful and uncompromising god had enlisted them as lieutenants in his ranks. This was not my god, nor that of most Jews. This was a warrior god, not a peaceful one. But then people have always shaped their gods in their own images. During the Crusades and the Inquisition, Jesus was a god of vengeance and barbarism. As is Allah during Jihad. And as is Jehovah on the West Bank.

The odd thing was that it all revealed a stunning lack of faith on the part of people who claimed to have so much of it. Surely the messiah was quite capable of making his own way, and didn't need all these people busily clearing the road for him by blowing it up. The truth was that they had a grievance with the messiah. He was taking too long to come, so they had to hurry him along. Blowing up the mosques would certainly create the big war they wanted — the war of Gog and Magog, of Armageddon. Then the messiah would have no choice but to come.

Messianism was not a spiritual matter for them, but a tactical one. *They,* not God, had the power to bring about the messiah. In fact, they had usurped the role of God. No matter how loud and how long they proclaimed themselves "the real Jews," they were no longer believing Jews at all, but idolaters. Bound into a narcissistic cult of superiority and violence, they became their own god.

Back in Jerusalem, I had talked to several people about what I had heard, hoping that the warning would be passed along and taken seriously in the right places. But the reaction to what I had to say had stumped me: "Oh, you shouldn't take them seriously. They're good boys, just a bit hotheaded. They get carried away when they talk to a pretty woman. It's all just talk and hot air. Pay no attention. You're too impressionable. You're just imagining things."

Six years later, after students had been gunned down at an Islamic seminary in Hebron, after two West Bank mayors had been crippled by car bombs, and after workers had been wounded by gunfire on buses, twenty-five Gush Emunim men were arrested on the eve of a planned attack on the Dome of the Rock and the El-Aqsa mosque. Three of them were among those I had talked to in 1978.

My sole consolation was that I was not the only one who had protested in vain. At the same time, liberal Knesset member Yossi Sarid had talked to everyone he could about the Jewish terrorist underground in the making. "It's all in your head," he was told. After the arrests in 1984 he could only say bitterly: "Now it's out of my head. Now it's in all our heads."

✡

Messianism hung heavy in the clear blue air of autumn Jerusalem as the terrorists' trial began. It would last well into the summer of 1985, when three were given life sentences and others received sentences of up to ten years. It became the Dreyfus trial of Israel, splitting the population between those who believed that the terrorists were right and should be let free, and those who believed that they should be given full punishment. Either way, there was no avoiding the issue. It even reached into popular songs. The ironic refrain of one song fast climbing the hit parade struck a harsh note in believing ears: "The messiah doesn't come, the messiah doesn't even call . . ."

The latest joke doing the rounds — so fast that for a time I was hearing it almost every day — was of the man who comes to a psychiatrist saying that he feels fine, but all his friends seem to think he needs help. "What seems to be the problem?" says the psychiatrist. "Well," says the man, "I don't know where to start." As is the way with psychiatrists, he is urged to "start at the beginning." With a shrug, he says: "All right. In the beginning, I created the heavens and the earth. . . ."

The ultranationalist right wing sprang to the defense of the terrorists on trial. They were neither criminals nor terrorists, even though all had pleaded guilty. They were good boys who had erred a little on the side of enthusiasm, wonderful boys who had gotten a bit carried away in their patriotism. They were the best of their generation, models for our youth, the defenders of Jewish women and children exposed to the stones of Palestinian rioters, men who had been left no choice but to take the law into their own hands. They deserved pardons, not life sentences. We should be proud of them instead of condemning them.

Thus went the popular defense. The argument was high on emotion, low on reason. These men had not taken the law into their own hands; they had taken guns and grenades and explosives into their own hands. To maintain that their sincerity excused their actions was patently absurd; Palestinian terrorists were just as sincere in their intentions, yet nobody in Israel would dream of calling them wonderful boys. And though the right wing objected to their even being called terrorists, that is what they were, brothers in arms with their Palestinian enemies. A blind belief in the justice of violence does not make anyone good; it makes them dangerous. When you take racism, add violence, and then mix it with the heady stuff of messianism, you have — literally — dynamite.

The racism is as crude as anywhere in the world. Sometimes it is familiar: "I was in the bank yesterday and this filthy old Arab comes walking in with a sack full of money. Cash. So where did he get his hands on all that money? What's he got to complain about? He's making plenty out of us." Other times it has an ancient biblical gloss: the Arabs are said to be the descendants of the evil race of Amalek and therefore, as one Gush Emunim rabbi argued in a booklet titled "The Mitzvah of Genocide in the Torah," they should all be wiped out.

There is much discussion within Gush Emunim as to whether Arabs should not be simply enslaved rather than wiped out. The slave-masters are the liberals of the movement. Ya'ir met one of them during a spell of reserve army service not long before. His unit had been assigned, despite protests, to guard a new Gush Emunim settlement on the hills above Hebron — the fate of commando fighters over age forty. In the middle of the night he had been visited by a young settler, submachine gun over his shoulder, on his own private patrol. The settler offered Ya'ir a drink of water and began talking effusively about his mission in life. "They are our slaves," he said, waving a thin grandiose arm over the Arab city below him. "It's written in the Bible: five slaves to each one of us. Because we are their superiors, historically and genetically. We are made to be their masters."

Ya'ir poured the water onto the ground in demonstration of his disgust. "Really?" he said, looking at the sunken chest, the wispy beard, the tiny eyes behind thick spectacles. "Tell me, when was the last time you ever looked in the mirror? Was that the master race you saw there?"

But sarcasm makes as little impact as reason. Fanaticism has its own dynamic. Still puzzling over how that dynamic worked, I had lunch with Tamara, a sociologist and civil rights activist who had known Dan Be'eri, the "philosopher" of the terrorist network, in Paris in the sixties. He had been a student at the Sorbonne then, radically left-wing, and not Jewish. Then the 1967 war ignited something in him, and he began to study Hebrew. Soon he converted to Judaism. He moved to Israel and gravitated to the Rav Kook Yeshiva in Jerusalem, the philosophical and organizational breeding ground of Gush Emunim. By the seventies he was living in the Gush Emunim township of Kiryat Arba, above Hebron. There he became a rabbi, started a school that taught everything except mathematics through the Bible, and became one of the most respected minds in the Jewish West Bank.

"He was extreme," said Tamara, "so perhaps it just didn't matter which extreme he was at. If he abandoned the radical left, he had nowhere to go but to the radical right."

You could call Dan Be'eri another victim of the '67 war — he and his victims in turn. Or perhaps he was a victim of history, unable to accept that what happened three or four thousand years ago in this place cannot determine what happens in the present. People like Be'eri are blind to the present. They live only for the past — the times of the Bible — and for the future, which will be the times of the messiah.

The whole idea of a messianic future is, of course, the stuff of drama, and it exerts a strong pull on those seeking to act out private pasts. Timid-eyed, wispy-bearded American youths come to Israel after years of fear, caution and ambivalence about their Jewishness, and suddenly light up with a newfound fervor: not only is it okay to be a Jew, but they can change the world's future by being one. A disproportionately large number of the Gush Emunim settlers are post-1967 immigrants like Be'eri. They never dreamed of coming to the small Israel that existed before; they were only attracted to the idea of being part of a strong, powerful Jewish state. Most of these immigrants came from the United States and the Soviet Union, making the West Bank perhaps the one place in the world where Americans and Russians see eye to eye. A peculiarly high number of them are converts, and many more are born-again Jews eager to make good on their newfound religiousness in the most demonstrative way possible.

Even as Tamara and I talked about them, one walked into the restaurant where we sat. The beard, the knitted yarmulke, the submachine gun over his shoulder, all made him unmistakable. "Is this restaurant kosher?" he asked in broken Hebrew.

It was a pointless question; you have to search out the non-kosher restaurants in West Jerusalem. Nobody bothered to answer. Tamara looked up at him in annoyance. "Here we don't eat with guns," she said. "Leave it outside or in the kitchen."

He looked at her in genuine puzzlement. "Excuse me, but do you speak English?"

She just shook her head in amazement, and then in bitterness. "How's he going to know his messiah when he comes?" she asked. "He doesn't even speak his language."

Another American, only a few months in Israel, had joined a yeshiva provocatively set up in the Moslem Quarter of the Old City, and rented a room in the Christian Quarter nearby. On Easter Saturday that year, which was also Shabbat, a Syrian Orthodox procession returning from services at the Holy Sepulchre had paused beneath his window, headed by a troop of boy scouts playing drums. The drums drove him mad with anger; they were an intolerable desecration of the holiness of his Sabbath day. So he had poured a cauldron of boiling water onto the boys in the street below. Five were taken to hospital for treatment for burns. More were injured in the ensuing fracas as the adults in the procession charged into the house to find the attacker. A police file was opened against him, but when it was made clear that they too would be charged for counterattacking, the Arabs filed no charges.

Once, such a thing would have been an isolated incident. But as incident began to follow incident, secular Israelis looked on in helpless despair. Gershom Schocken, editor of the prestigious *Ha'aretz*, wrote flatly of an Israel sliding back into the Middle Ages in language that just a few years before would have been that of the radical opposition. Another newspaper editor slumped sadly in his office chair. "I've been in this country fifty years," he said, spreading his bare arms wide and staring at them as though his whole life were contained in that burly span, "and in all that fifty years, I have never,

never been so saddened and so concerned about the state of the country and its future. It's like *1984* from the other side. In the novel, it was Communist totalitarianism. Here, it's heading for right-wing nationalist totalitarianism, mystical and fascist.''

In the seventies, this man had been considered right of center. He hadn't changed; the center had. Like Schocken, and Oded, and Dan — like almost all the journalists I know here — he knows too much to be quiet, yet cannot write without terrible pain. And part of that pain is the increasing awareness of how little real influence he has. Among this People of the Book, he is learning the futility of the written word.

An ancient, fanatical Jerusalem seems to be reasserting itself. A medieval morality play is being acted out in flying stones and boiling water — a cruel parody of the kabbalistic vision of Jerusalem as the sexual union of heaven and earth through stone and water.

"The air above Jerusalem is saturated with prayers and dreams. / Like the air above industrial towns / It's hard to breathe,'' Amichai once wrote. Perhaps the new Jerusalem we thought we'd built had been an impossible dream. This city's entire past consists of the unholy alliance of religion and politics. Gush Emunim is yet another in the long line of messianic movements that has been the subtext of Jewish history for thousands of years.

For a while it had been easy to be romantic about religion, even as it gathered its ancient political force around me. Clues of the heavenly Jerusalem in the earthly one were the exotic counterpoint to my life here. There was a mystic undercurrent to the city — a kind of recessed lighting that gave shadows and depth to everyday life.

But the Godly ice cream van had lost its glow, and the tears of the archangel Gabriel now seemed as hard as bullets. "They're taking this city away from us," Tamara was saying. "They're taking the whole country away from us."

I nodded dumbly. All this talk of messiahs was exhausting. Perhaps you need to be religious to withstand it. You certainly need to be religious to avoid the bitter knowledge of one of the oldest pieces of Jewish lore, paraphrased appropriately by Franz Kafka: "The messiah will only come when he is no longer needed."

Kafka's was the voice of doubt. But there is no doubt in the minds of the messianists. They don't want peace, and they say so; they want great events. They don't want rest; they want redemption. They are the extreme development of the thirst for excitement that still racks this country, leading to delusions as powerful as those swirling through the mind of someone dying of thirst in the desert.

I took a deep draught from the glass in front of me and watched morosely as the waiter placed hummus and eggplant and tehina salads on the table between Tamara and me. "God save us from saviors, from messiahs of all kinds," I thought. "They are the ones who'll destroy us."

X

BLACK-AND-WHITE pictures flickered on the screen. Everyone in them was smiling. Two dashing young fighters named Moshe Dayan and Yigal Allon posed by their horses with careless grins. Girls with dark romantic eyes tended sheep. Young men set up "tower-and-fence" settlements overnight, trucking in prefabricated walls. ("So that's how they did it," murmured Ya'ir beside me.) People marched in protest against the British White Paper limiting Jewish immigration. Refugee boats arrived off the Tel Aviv shore. Actors declaimed in the old eastern European style of the early Habimah Theater. (A grand old man of the Israeli stage, seated the other side of me, stirred in his seat and nodded at his screen image.) Ben-Gurion read out the Declaration of Independence. Yemenites kissed the ground on arriving at Lod airport. Youthful writers smoked and drank around a tiny café table on Dizengoff Street. (One of them, white hair standing out from his head Ben-Gurion-style, chuckled softly behind me.) Palmach fighters on horseback came charging down a sand dune. Politicians flicked flies from their noses as the first Independence Day parade went by. (The audience laughed as affectionately as it had years before.)

They were clips from old movie-house newsreels, shown at the Cinemateque in honor of Nathan Axelrod. Throughout the thirties and the forties and on into the fifties, he had quietly gone about his task of making the newsreels shown before the main attraction. Now, in the eighties, *he* was the main attraction, and this was a gala showing of his work.

Mayor Teddy Kollek presented him with a medal "showing all the beauty of Jerusalem." The whole hall full of people strained forward to catch a glimpse of the medal, unable to imagine how it could possibly contain so much. Perhaps it was a magic medal, with an infinite capacity to show you whatever it was you were seeking.

We watched the old newsreels for an hour and a half. I could have watched through to the next morning, and then some. There was the intimacy of the tiny state in the making. Everyone on the screen seemed to be saying: "Look, this is ours, we created it, we *are* it!"

Nobody could just go home afterward. A few of us ended up in my room at Mishkenot, and talked far into the night over a table laden with whatever I could find in the kitchen: salad and goat cheese, crackers and bread, grapes, dried apricots, wine, whiskey, Turkish coffee . . .

"Those movies made me feel sad," Ya'ir was saying. "They made me want to cry for what has become of such great drama and energy. They were so sure of themselves then, sure they were making history. And look at what we've done with it." He was born into those times, in 1941. His parents had been part of them. But he felt a sense of immense distance.

"So much promise and whatever happened to it?" said Nira, nodding soulfully over her glass. "So much promise gone to waste. Then what was the use of all that energy and innocence? Does it seem better at a distance? Was it really that way?"

I was puzzled, then confused and even a little angry. I

couldn't take their pessimism, probably because it was a mirror of my own. They were stealing my lines. "You talk as though you were the ones who'd left," I said, "not me. There's no point in comparison. If you compare the country now to the country then, you're comparing two different things. It's a false way of looking at history. And besides, we were watching movies, not reality. They were newsreels, made to make people feel good about what was going on." Made to create the nostalgia we were all feeling.

Geula was sitting very quietly meanwhile — unusual for her. She was smiling with the faraway look of memory. She was in her late fifties now, but she still had the energy and enthusiasm of youth, and the same artistic flamboyance. "How did those newsreels make *you* feel?" I asked.

She thought a moment, and then in her deep throaty voice said: "Proud." Slowly, as though tasting the sound of that word, she said it again: "Yes, they made me feel proud." I wanted to kiss her for that. "After all," she went on, "we did create a country."

She had taken part in those protests, had joined the Haganah, had lived fully in those times. However idealized the version we had seen on the screen, it had still been real, it had still happened. "Look, after all, we're here," said Geula.

Ya'ir and Nira and myself, all circling forty, were either unborn or infants at the time, and we were far more bitter than she — bitter for an idealized time we never knew firsthand. Perhaps it is always easier to look back thirty or forty years and see things as simpler and purer then. Perhaps those who were not there are doomed to the strange fate of always harking back to a better past, saying, "Things were different then, and if only . . ." It is easy to do, when you never knew the hard side of that past.

I thought of Yehoshafat Harkabi, once head of Israeli army

intelligence and now a political science professor at the Hebrew University. In the late sixties, when I was studying for my second degree in psychology, he had given a seminar on simulation games and role-playing, and one day he had taken us slowly, verbally, through what it was like to be a Palestinian born into one of the refugee camps in Jordan or southern Lebanon. We were fed from infancy on the heady myth of Palestine as a land of milk and honey, a land where all was perfect, where one could live on figs and dates and oranges plucked fresh from the tree, where the jasmine was the most fragrant in the world, the water the sweetest, the life the most idyllic until shattered by the Israelis in 1948. For the sons and daughters of the original refugees — for the generation born in exile — the idea of Palestine had a far stronger pull than did the real land for their parents, who had known its harshness.

Now, as I made more coffee for everyone in my room at Mishkenot, it occurred to me that we too looked nostalgically to a past we never knew, bitterly comparing an idealized image to what we knew today.

Yitzhak seemed indifferent to it all. He had only arrived from the Soviet Union a couple of years before. His concern was coming to terms with the Israel that existed now, not the one that had been. "And you," said Geula, big dark eyes turning the spotlight on me, "what did you feel?"

Now it was my turn to pause and search for words. "Fascinated," I said. "And affectionate too. And grateful, I think, to those people and their energy. And also, I admired them. They made a positive kind of history. As you said, they created something. And that's especially important to me right now because I sometimes think that the country's developed a negative energy instead, a destructive one. Maybe the past is an indication of what we still could be."

Yet as the night turned into the early hours of the morning, I could almost imagine that time had not moved at all. I was happy just to be with this crowd of people around the table, drinking and eating, laughing and arguing. Ya'ir was slouched on the steps leading down into the dining area and I watched him, smiling, wondering how it was that whenever one of us had been free, the other had always been involved with someone else. Yet here he was now, divorced, and here I was, due to leave in another few weeks. What was possible in the past was too late now. He returned my gaze, smiling too.

Geula and Yitzhak began an impassioned discussion about why Russian immigrants seemed so attracted to the extreme right. A wave of tiredness came over me. I was a little drunk; we all were. I took the combs out of my hair, letting it down, and stretched lazily. Ya'ir rose to say good night. He came over and put his arm around my head, so that I leaned into him. It felt natural and comfortable, as though we'd been making love all afternoon.

"I'll see you to the gate," I said, and we walked along the terrace hand in hand. The night was fresh and cool, the moon full again. At the gate, it seemed a shame to part, so I walked down into the valley with him, and across the bridge to the point where steps lead to the path up Mount Zion. And there at the foot of Mount Zion we kissed and laughed and kissed again.

"You know, I sometimes wondered how come we never got together," I said. "There's time now," he replied. And the night was suddenly warm as we parted and I went back through Yemin Moshe to Mishkenot.

The place was empty of people. Both doors were open, front and back, and light shone out welcomingly onto the terrace. I hadn't realized how long I'd been away. I'd make my apologies in the morning. But meanwhile, as I began to wash the dishes and the glasses, I had a feeling of rightness in this world, at this moment, in this place. I had been back a month.

That night, as the trees outside the window cast moon shadows over my face, I slept the sleep of an old innocence.

✡

We didn't have to call each other. The next Friday morning we bumped into each other in town, both of us laden down with newspapers and groceries. "Come over later and we'll have lunch on the terrace," I said. Ya'ir nodded: "I'll bring hummus and wine." It wasn't a combination that had ever occurred to me.

He arrived as I finished reading the papers, the newsprint of three or four publications strewn around me on the flagstones. He brought with him hummus from Ta'ami, with whole chickpeas heaped on top of the paste and a generous supply of hot-pepper sauce; Adom Atik wine, the vin ordinaire of Israel that far surpasses most of the more expensive labels; and to my surprise, since Israeli men are not known as the great romantics of this world, flowers. I made an Israeli salad, chopping up tomatoes, onions, cucumbers and parsley and sprinkling the mix with oil and lemon juice, pepper and salt, and we sat outside to eat.

The traffic below Mount Zion began to thin out as the center of town emptied and the air became lazy with the peace of a Friday afternoon. It was the most relaxed time of the week, the time when you have the whole of Shabbat ahead of you. Stores close at one, people linger for an hour or two in the Tsrif or on Ben-Yehuda Street, and then all Jerusalem goes quiet, basking in the sun, waiting for nightfall and the Friday evening meal.

We talked about Shai's farm out in the hills to the west of

the city. Shai had been one of Jerusalem's "characters" in the sixties — always stoned or drunk, knowing everybody, with a crazy laugh that could be heard wafting over the crowd at any party you went to. And then right after the '73 war he had disappeared. Gone off into the hills, people said. Found an old hut and set up home there. Made an arrangement with the Jewish National Fund to be a forest watchman.

I had been out to see him there not long before. Over the years, he'd added to the hut and started a farm, raising goats and horses and chickens. He had married and started a family too. Visiting Shai that day had been like walking into another, more peaceful world — a world set amid sage and thornbushes in the silence of the hills. It was the Jerusalem version of how Big Sur once was, or Woodstock: the self-sufficient life, alone and peaceful. The old crazy Shai had been transformed.

As I'd helped him milk the goats, he'd seemed solid and calm. He talked about the new breed he was developing, selling the males off to kibbutzim, where they would sire new herds. His kibbutz friends had tried to persuade him to breed hundreds of goats instead of the twenty he had, but as he said, laughing, "What would I do with all those goats? I'd have to become an industry!"

Shai's peace had recently been threatened by a plan to build an Israel Defense Forces museum over a thousand acres of a nearby hill, spilling over to include his tiny farm. Ya'ir and a few others had quietly gotten together to see what they could do. They had talked to the architect, who hadn't even realized that Shai came within the borders of his new project. And now, as we finished our meal, Ya'ir told me that it would be okay: "The architect agrees with us: if there's no room for a Shai out there in the hills, then there's no room left for any of us in this country."

Over the wine, Ya'ir and I began to talk about retreat. It was the Yom Kippur War that had sent Shai out into the hills, despairing of what he had seen, or despairing of the despair that had descended on the whole country in the months after that war. Ya'ir too had thought about leaving at that time. His brother had been killed in the war, he was struggling with survivor guilt, and there was no room for any illusion, as there had been after the '67 war, that this was the last war we'd see.

He had taken off into the hills on foot one day. He walked as far west as the hills would take him and reached Bab El-Wad, the spot where the Tel Aviv–Jerusalem road abruptly enters the mountains. There he climbed the hillside to the old Turkish watchtower where migrating storks nest in season. The storks were there, as he knew they would be. As the sun set, he sat there watching them and envying them, knowing that they'd leave, and knowing too that he would not.

I had my own memory of storks and war. Like Ya'ir's, it was the sharper for the old association of storks with birth. And like his, it too came with guilt.

It was in the second year of Israel's Lebanon war. A report in the *New York Times* mentioned gangs of young fighters whose latest sport was to go out into the hills above Beirut and empty their submachine guns in a frenzy of release at flocks of migrating storks flying overhead. I don't remember whether they were Shiites or Palestinians or Phalangists or any of the other divisions in Lebanon. I do remember being shocked by the wanton destructiveness and cruel glee. And then being shocked by that shock. People were being killed every day in Lebanon, and it seemed that I had reacted more to the death of storks.

"We all find our own means of defense," said Ya'ir, "our own peculiar means of living with what's happening. You can't

make judgments about how you react in situations like that."
Still, it would come as a comfort a few months later when I
read a piece in the *Times* by Pulitzer Prize–winner Tom
Friedman in which he recounted how the most vivid scene of
destruction for him had been when a Shiite fighter burst into
the bar of Beirut's Commodore Hotel and machine-gunned all
the bottles of liquor. Here was a man who had seen death and
destruction every day, yet it was the seemingly irrelevant scene
in the bar that struck home. Perhaps because it was so unexpected, it had released emotion previously suppressed —
emotion that Friedman almost had to suppress if he was to go
on living and working under such circumstances.

"I'll take you down to Bab El-Wad one day," said Ya'ir,
"next time you're here. There are no storks there right now."
He looked at me. "After all, you will be coming back, won't
you?" It wasn't really a question.

I gave a sheepish grin. "It doesn't look like I'm much good
at staying away. It's odd, but despite everything that's happening here, I still feel . . . I feel right when I'm here, like
somehow this is my place."

He nodded, smiling. *"Nino'ach,"* he said. I didn't know
the word in Hebrew. "More than comfortable," he explained, searching for the right expression and then finding it:
"At home."

I might have argued that point, but between us, at least,
there was something very *nino'ach.* We made love slowly and
gently as the gold of late afternoon deepened into darkness,
and slept peacefully that night, in a New Zealand of our own
making.

XI

"**J**EZEBEL! Jezebel! Fornicating under God's holy mountain!''

The words came floating back at me across the years, though the little man with the trim black Hitler-style mustache had long gone. He had jumped up and down by the windmill as he shouted at me, flailing his arms as though trying to encourage the broken mill to start working again, and looking back and forth from Mount Zion to me to make it quite clear which Jezebel he meant, and which holy mountain.

He had been part of the neighborhood in those years. Everybody was so used to him that nobody thought to warn me, and this first encounter took me by surprise. The neighborhood children scrambled up onto walls for the spectacle, mimicking him from a safe distance — a row of little windmills yelling "Jezebel!" — until finally he gave up on me and began to throw stones at them, and the whole scene dissipated in a flurry of shrieks, giggles and skittering stones.

"It's his nerves," explained my next-door neighbor, who was from Turkey. That was the Middle Eastern way of saying that he was quite mad.

Nobody really noticed at what point he disappeared; it just occurred to us one day that we hadn't seen him in a while. He was probably taken to a mental hospital — to the grand old mansion in Talbieh, perhaps, where patients sit in the swings of the nearby rose garden and urinate noisily onto the ground through the wooden slats, or to the one in Givat Sha'ul on the outskirts of the city that used to be the village of Dir Yassin, the scene of the 1948 massacre of Arab civilians that haunts both Palestinian memory and Menachem Begin's reputation.

I might have forgotten him altogether and left him to the limbo of the mental patient if sexuality were not such a strong undercurrent to the conflict here. In the heavenly Jerusalem, that is attractive: the old kabbalistic idea is that the world is kept alive by the coupling of the Shechinah and the King, the female and male aspects of the Godhead, once a month on the Temple Mount. But that's a mystical idea, part of the prettiness of old legends. It all becomes far less pretty in reality.

Daniella was once more than pretty. She had been stunningly beautiful, and even now cut a striking figure, tall and rangy, with dark features and a mass of curly black hair falling over her shoulders. She was from one of the elite Sephardic families, the ones who trace their lineage directly from Spain, and had married a good, reliable but perhaps just too solid Ashkenazic man. At times she seemed like a character from an Israeli novel of the fifties — a wild exotic beauty penned in behind the fences of respectability. One had the impression of a bird with clipped wings, always about to fly yet not quite knowing how.

She came around to see me one morning, bearing a plate of figs, an invitation to dinner the next evening, and an intense curiosity about what I was doing on this visit. I answered vaguely, as writers do, when she asked what this book was about, and then seeing her disappointment, added jokingly that I did know one thing about it: it would include all the best places in Jerusalem to make love outdoors. But instead of laughing as I expected, she frowned in concern. "You shouldn't do that," she said.

"Why not?" I asked, thinking that after all it was not such a bad idea. There is something about outdoors love that makes the place peculiarly yours, creating a bond of intensity between person and landscape.

"But don't you realize that Arabs will read this book?"

I hadn't really thought about it, and failed to see her point. "Arab *men*," she emphasized. "They'll read it, and you know their culture is very different from ours, and they'll come ringing at your door expecting you to go out to all those places and do it with them."

I burst out laughing. "Daniella, you can't be serious," I began. And then abruptly stopped laughing as I saw from her face that she was. I wanted badly to change the subject. Very badly. "Never mind," I said quickly, "I was just kidding."

We talked of other things, but I couldn't shake from my mind what she'd said. It was something long hidden, something that once smouldered beneath the surface, revealed only in odd brilliant flashes like the controversial imagery of the Amos Oz novel *My Michael*. There the woman protagonist, slowly losing her mind, fantasizes about the Arab twins she played with as a child, long before the 1948 War of Independence. They have now become terrorists in her mind, and they move through her fantasies with a strong, violent sexual aura.

Now this sexual obsession with the enemy had crept up to the surface of Israeli society. It was an attraction to and fear of "the Arab," a complex obsession not unlike that of whites with black sexual power in the Deep South of fifty or a hundred years ago. Even the reactions were from an earlier time: when a mentally disturbed Arab man lifted the skirt of a Jewish woman in the Hebron market and asked her to marry him, she promptly fainted.

It was still on Daniella's mind at dinner the next evening. I was talking with someone from the Hebrew University School of Education about Neve Shalom, the small privately funded Arab-Jewish settlement between Jerusalem and Tel Aviv — the only one of its kind — where an experimental school had just started up. Daniella listened with open mouth. "You mean . . . they're learning together?" she asked in the shocked tones of someone wanting only to be told that she had heard wrong. "Arab and Jewish children, in the same classroom, learning together?" She could not have sounded more shocked if we had told her that the five-year-olds were copulating together under the olive trees.

"What's so shocking about that?" I asked. "What's there to be against?"

"Oh, but I *am* against it," she said fervently. "Absolutely against it! We have to concentrate on ourselves, we Jews, when we're surrounded by enemies. We need a Jewish identity, and we can't afford to get it mixed up in something like this. What will become of these children, tell me? Just think of the effect this will have on them. How could anyone think of such a thing?"

"I could understand perhaps if you said you didn't want your own children to go to such a school," said the educator. "But to oppose the school itself . . ."

"Listen," said Daniella, "I'm not a racist, but . . ." But the Jews must look to their own education first. But the Jews couldn't afford such intimacy with their enemies. But such education would lead to intermarriage. . . .

Now it was I who was shocked. The worst thing I could have said about Neve Shalom was that it was an isolated and somewhat naive attempt, but it was certainly eminently worthy. I had been invited to go down there and spend a morning watching classes but had turned down the invitation, saying that I didn't want to stand and marvel at how wonderful it was that Arabs and Jews should learn together because since one out of every six Israelis is Arab, they should be learning together in every school in the country. But now I began to regret that high-minded refusal. When such a seemingly innocuous idea raises such deeply emotional opposition, astonishment and praise may be the only sensible reactions.

The sexual fear in Daniella's racism was clear enough. Neither that nor the racism itself was uniquely Israeli; they seem to be the scourge of every country on this earth, throughout the third world as well as the first. But I was pained because I too was Israeli, and because I could see the scourge spreading.

✡

The star of the most popular movie in release that fall was Mohammed Bakri. Tall, gaunt and blue-eyed, he is one of the new generation of Israeli Arabs moving gradually into the mainstream of the country in one of the classic minority ways. The movie was *Behind the Bars* (released abroad as *Beyond the Walls*), a tale of Arab and Jewish prisoners in the same jail who realize in the course of the movie that it is in their joint interest to cooperate against a corrupt prison administration.

It was a well-made movie and had already won a special Critics' Award at the Venice Film Festival, where a telling confusion took place during the press conference following the awards ceremony. Bakri's Jewish co-star Arnon Tzadok is short and swarthy; the organizers decided that he must therefore be the Arab star, and seated him behind Bakri's nameplate. The tall blue-eyed Bakri, they thought, must be the new breed of Israeli Jew, and he was accordingly placed behind Tzadok's nameplate.

Despite the Venice prize, the movie quickly became controversial in Israel. After it had been in release for four weeks, the Knesset Education Committee decided to ban any part of it from being shown on the state-run television, on the grounds that it delivered a subversive message. They acted too late, and the movie played to packed houses throughout the country for months. The hopeful saw its popularity as a sign of a changing tide; the cynical maintained that it was merely enthusiasm for a good thriller that didn't need subtitles.

One woman who went to see the movie had undergone an operation for cancer not long before. She thought the film good, though the violence of the language disturbed her somewhat. She saw no particular political message in it; it was just another movie. But that night, a dream told her otherwise. She dreamed she was in a bus, and behind her in the bus sat Mohammed Bakri. She leaned back against him, and he began to fondle her from behind. As his hands cupped her breasts, she felt herself moving against him, wanting him.

Abruptly, she woke in terror. She rushed to the bathroom and vomited, and then took a shower. Still feeling dirty, she took another one. By dawn, she had been in and out of the shower five times. She told a friend about the dream the next morning. "Now I understand why I have cancer," she said. "It's the Arabs. They've invaded my mind. They've implanted their cancer in my body."

The cancerous association was not new. There had been a minor furor when the general in charge of Northern Command, "Yanush" Ben-Gal, had called Israeli Arabs "a cancer in the body of the State of Israel." That was in 1978, when to say such a thing was still cause for scandal. But since the rabidly racist Meir Kahane had been elected to the Knesset in the summer of 1984, such crude metaphors had become increasingly common. A hothouse climate had developed in which sexual fears could be expressed, and not only among women.

A Jewish woman involved in Israeli-Palestinian peace efforts told me of Jewish boyfriends who asked with great curiosity if she had ever been to bed with an Arab. "What was it like?" was the all-important question. She told them it was the best sex she had ever known, and showed them the door.

Sometimes male fears are disguised homosexual fantasies. One soldier went AWOL for a few days and spent the time sunning himself in Eilat. On his return to camp, he told his officers that he had been kidnapped and raped by Arabs, spinning a picturesque story: they had sprayed him with a sleeping potion, and the next thing he knew, he was waking up in an alley off Jerusalem's Jaffa Road "with his clothes in disarray and his trousers undone." The story was transparent enough, not least because he had been seen in Eilat; he was sentenced to a spell in military jail, and demoted from corporal to private.

In such a climate, when even the most unlikely events become combustible material, a sexual murder is the equivalent of a gallon of kerosene poured onto the flames. And that fall, Hadass Kedmi was murdered.

She was a young woman soldier who had disappeared while hitchhiking home to her Galilee kibbutz from army camp. The search for her went on for two weeks, but even before the body was found, suspicion fell on Israeli Arabs. When residents of Arab villages near her kibbutz helped out in the search, there was a highly publicized confrontation between the head of the Border Police and the Haifa chief of police over the

Arabs' participation. "Leave the Arabs out of this," said the Border Police chief. "They're all murderers."

When they found her in the hills outside Haifa, Hadass Kedmi had been savagely and repeatedly raped and beaten before being killed. There was no evidence to indicate who might have done it, and nobody was arrested. But the popular press went to town with comparisons to other sexual murders. They played up the recent Cremisan murders, for which David Ben-Shimol had taken his ugly revenge, as well as the abduction, murder and sexual mutilation of fourteen-year-old Danny Katz a year before, for which four young Israeli Arabs were about to stand trial, charged with "a combination of sexual and nationalistic motives."

Israeli Arabs cowered under the suspicion, convinced that any murder of a Jew, especially if combined with sexual violence, would now indict them. Their resentment grew as they suspected police of ignoring murders of Arabs. An Arab youth had disappeared from his Galilee home about three months before, and a firm belief had taken root that he had been abducted and killed by Kahane's "boys." One man in a village near Kedmi's kibbutz asked a reporter: "Are Israel's Arabs hostages who have to justify themselves and prove their innocence again and again?"

The question, as he knew all too well, was rhetorical. But then rhetoric is a favored mode of expression in this part of the world. And here, no words stay empty for long.

A few months later, a Jewish taxi driver was murdered in East Jerusalem. The police announced that they suspected the motive was terrorism. They were wrong; a week later, when three Arab suspects were arrested, it became clear that the motive had been robbery. But the words had already been spoken, and the seeds of revenge already sown. A few more days, and three young Jews took a taxi from East Jerusalem to Maaleh Adumim, the huge new suburb in the Judean desert. There, they shot the Arab driver three times from a distance of one foot. "Kahane is right," they said when arrested. "This is the only way."

✡

"I say what you think!" Kahane screams to a crowd of underprivileged Sephardic youths in a dusty development town. They roar back their approval. His face contorted, teeth bared, fists waving, Kahane in performance has the look of a rabid dog. Sometimes he even foams at the mouth.

As his yellow-shirted "boys" work the crowd into a frenzy · of slogan chanting — "Arabs out!" "A clean Israel!" "Kaha-ne!" — he can be raging one moment and in tears the next. The tears are a calculated part of working the crowd, raising high the level of emotion.

There is something of parody about him. But then the old newsreels of Hitler's speeches can also seem like a horrifying parody of human behavior, distorted and mocked by some cruel puppet-master pulling the most primitive strings.

The crowd loves Kahane. His bills have been rejected by the establishment — in fact, thrown out of the Knesset, as many had hoped that he himself would be. But here in the streets, Kahane is king.

His rhetoric grinds out violence, manipulating the fear of Arabs into a gut hatred. He plays up the sexual fear for all it's worth, and has just announced that he'll be going to Arab villages to make Jewish wives leave their Arab husbands. (The handful of such marriages are the focus of a constant low-grade prurient fascination.) "They're seducing the daughters of Israel!" he screams. "They're corrupting our race, polluting our women! Protect your families, Jews! Rise up and defend the purity of your daughters!'' He goes straight for the balls, for the most raw emotions. The eyes of his followers, mostly young Americans and Moroccans, shine with lust — blood lust.

On her way to the supermarket in Gilo, the new suburb between Jerusalem and Bethlehem, my friend Nira passed by another Kahane performance. She heard the rhetoric and saw the rapt faces of the crowd. Scared, she turned into the market, and there at the back came face to face with the Arab stockroom boy. They looked each other in the eye for a moment; he turned away in fear, she in shame.

She could no longer deny the problem, as she had for years. Kahane had brought it right up front. And the irony is that if he can spur Israelis to horror and shame — and to action against him because of those feelings — he may achieve more for Israel's democracy than could hundreds of well-intentioned speeches in the Knesset.

As support for Kahane grows, so too does organized opposition to him. When he announced that he would demonstrate outside the Jerusalem movie house showing *Behind the Bars,* for example, the scout movement organized against him. Fourteen-year-old Amir, David and Ilana's youngest, was a scout leader; he was going to take his whole troop to the counterdemonstration. I said I'd come too, but I had to go to a wedding first and got away too late. Amir told me the story of his first political battle later that evening.

There had been about twenty people with Kahane, all burly youths clearly spoiling for a fight. But there had been more than three hundred counterdemonstrators, mainly from the scouts, who kept up a chant of ''Racism will not pass!'' so persistently that Kahane could not be heard. A single tomato flew through the air and caught Kahane in the eye, and the astonished crowd then saw Kahane and his troupe fleeing down a side alley, routed.

For a while, Kahane kept mainly to the development towns and the suburbs, the places where resentment breeds and he can feed off it. That resentment is both particularly Israeli and historically familiar. Establishment commentators now draw the comparisons as a matter of routine. The constantly deteriorating economic situation (with the Israeli shekel worth one seven-hundred-and-fiftieth of its equivalent in 1977, when Menachem Begin came to power) seemed to parallel the rapid rise of support for Kahane (quadrupled since he had been in the Knesset), and those two factors were too similar to conditions in Germany during the early thirties to be ignored. Veteran journalist Ya'ir Kotler published a biography of Kahane. It was not an authorized biography, and those who most needed to read it never would. It was called *Heil Kahane!*

✡

Kahane's ideas are painfully familiar. All Arabs — both those who are Israeli citizens and those who live in the occupied territories — should be either paid to leave or forcibly expelled. All Jews who disagree with him are either "self-hating Jews" (the phrase used as a knee-jerk reaction to any criticism from Jews) or traitors, and they should be expelled, imprisoned, or simply killed. It should be a criminal offense, meanwhile, for a Jew and a non-Jew to have sexual relations, for a non-Jew to live within the boundaries of Jerusalem, and for Jews and non-Jews to use the same public facilities.

In the fall of 1984, polls showed that although more than half the Israeli public absolutely opposed these ideas, more than a quarter thought there was a lot of sense in them. Kahane's popularity continued to soar, despite a Knesset decision designed specifically to ban his party from standing in the next elections. "The youth are mine," he said, and it looked as though he was right. A study of fifteen- to eighteen-year-olds by the prestigious Van Leer Institute in Jerusalem showed that about one-third of Israeli youths were democratic in their thinking, one-quarter antidemocratic, and the rest mixed in their thinking, depending on the issue at hand. Sixty percent of the young people thought that Israeli Arabs should not have equal rights; 62 percent wanted to annex the West Bank outright; 44 percent thought there should be a law against press criticism of government policy. These findings were weighted by one special factor: while secular youth were largely democratic in values, religious youth were heavily antidemocratic.

Support or oppose him, Kahane now had to be seriously reckoned with. Five years before, he had been seen as a madman, an irrelevant American import to the Israeli political scene. But as the whole tone of the country moved to the right under Begin, he became what one commentator acidly called "reasonable lunacy" — and then an acceptable part of Israeli politics. What had begun as an illness had become an epidemic.

Its effects were clear by the summer of 1985, especially in the southern Galilee town of Afula after two Jewish schoolteachers were found murdered on nearby Mount Gilboa. The townspeople went on an anti-Arab rampage, beating up any Arab they could find (as well as a Jew they mistook for an Arab). At the teachers' funerals, the terrifying chant was "Kahane, Kahane — Messiah, Messiah!"

Now each additional poll showed increasing electoral support for Kahane. After the funeral, one poll estimated that he could get almost 10 percent of the vote. And then there were the results of the latest Van Leer Institute survey of Israeli youth, in which 42 percent said they supported Kahane. Among religious youth, the support shot up to 60 percent.

I called the chief researcher, and together we explored the

possible explanations for such shocking figures. There was the tendency of teenagers the world over to go for extremist solutions to complex problems. There was the fact that these young people had grown up since 1967 with a double message — democracy inside Israel proper, and no democracy in the territories — which they had taken to mean democracy for Jews and no democracy for Arabs, no matter whether those Arabs were Israeli citizens or residents of occupied territory. And there was a backlash reaction to the abject failure of Israel's Lebanon war, leading to the simplistic idea that if you just got rid of all the Arabs, you would get rid of Israel's problems.

"You're sighing?" asked the researcher as we went over the findings.

"Sure, I'm sighing. What did *you* do when you saw these figures? Forty-two percent support Kahane, fifty-three percent oppose him; it's getting to be a frighteningly even battle."

"Don't worry," he replied. "In the battle between the sons of light and the sons of darkness, you know who will win."

I sighed again. "I wish I did."

I put down the phone and went back to the papers on my desk. There was the first report of the Van Leer Institute's new school program, "Education for Democracy," which focused on teachers' reactions to the program and their own struggles with themselves over its content. Beside it were my notes from a seminar held at the institute on relations between Arabs and Jews in Israel, "Between Two Cultures." The audience had been almost entirely Jewish — educators, psychologists, sociologists and students committed to bridging the gap. Their presence said they wanted coexistence and understanding. There were only a few faces of blank refusal.

As fate would have it, one of those few had sat down beside me. He had a smooth fleshy face with a certain boyish kind of handsomeness, and wore a knitted yarmulke. I'd looked at him from time to time, and received a blank stare of non-recognition in return. To judge by the papers on his lap, he was a student of education.

Rafik Halaby had been one of the speakers. He was a Druze television reporter and news editor who had survived a concerted attempt by the right wing to get him out of television news on the grounds that since he was Arab, his coverage of West Bank affairs was biased. "Some look for the enemy behind the man," he said that night, "while others look for the man behind the enemy." I looked again at my neighbor. He was reading a book, holding it demonstratively high so that he couldn't see Halaby's face. The book was called *Children's Perception of Death.*

XII

THERE is little greenery in the Jewish Quarter of the Old City. Religious law forbids the planting of anything but orchards, and there is no room for orchards in this claustrophobic maze of alleys. There is only the harshness of stone. Voices echo off it, feet ache on it, souls bruise on it.

The quarter was intended to be a mixed religious and secular neighborhood when it was renovated in the early seventies. But the secular had nearly all moved out, feeling hemmed in by religion and by all that stone. Among the few people I still knew who lived there were a young religious couple who were also liberal — no contradiction, but an increasingly rare combination in Israel today. I went to visit them one morning, and listened as they worried about what had happened to the quarter. But they couldn't conceive of moving out, and I could see why. It would mean abandoning the calm inner courtyard of their house, the domed rooms, and the almost magical sense of inner space in the midst of the crowded outer one.

As they made lunch, I went up onto the roof, taking in the classic view of the mosques and the Mount of Olives behind them. I began to do a few stretching exercises, tentatively trying out the damaged knee. It seemed to be holding. As I stretched, a boy appeared on the neighboring roof. He was four or five years old, perhaps, with the sidelocks and the black yarmulke of the Orthodox. He watched me in silence for a minute, and then began shouting at me — the same phrase, over and over again.

"Ruh min hon!" "Get out of here!"

Just three words. Not in Hebrew, but in Arabic. And since he said them incorrectly, they clearly were the only three words he knew in that language. It was a crude and insulting phrase, often used by non-Arabic-speaking Israelis to scatter the hordes of Arab kids trying to sell them chewing gum in the parking lot by Jaffa Gate. Over and over he screamed: *"Ruh min hon! Ruh min hon!"*

I was wearing jeans and a long loose shirt. He certainly did not think I was Arab. But he did see me as a stranger. I was alien: not one of his, not a religious Jew. And all others were as Arabs in his mind. All others should get out of here.

I let loose at him in Hebrew and he disappeared. The encounter left me angry. My friends, upset, calmed me down. But I was very glad to get out of the Jewish Quarter afterward, away from that closed-in feeling of walls upon walls. Coming out of Zion Gate, I walked the narrow alley between the Old City wall and the wall of the Armenian cemetery on Mount Zion to the point where both walls suddenly fall away to the open view over Gehenna and Yemin Moshe. I stood there breathing deep in relief. "Too many walls," I thought. "Too many walls."

To each their own environment. The mind — the spirit, the soul — finds its place, the one that suits it, where it feels good and can follow its own direction. The Orthodox found theirs in the closed confines of the Jewish Quarter, which had become a sterile place for self-righteous souls who see little joy in Judaism. I found mine here, looking out over hills and space into the far distance. Better by far to look at those battlement walls from the outside than to be inside them, embattled.

Safely outside, back at Mishkenot, I sat on the terrace reading Graham Greene, the high priest of doubt. Here was a writer who found the heart of the matter in the regions of borders. His characters were in foreign countries, close to foreign borders. Physical uprootedness was his symbol of doubt. He was a good person to read at the edge of what had once been no-man's-land. And perhaps a bad person to read in a land claimed by too many people. Sometimes this whole country seems to me so burdened by the number of claims on it that it becomes unclaimable. "Because it's ours," "Because it was promised to us," "Because our great-great-grandfathers were born here" — these claimant phrases make a fetish of this stony land. The fact of ownership becomes more important than the land itself.

Yet I too had that proprietary sense. I felt it especially as I went walking around Yemin Moshe, checking out the changes, searching in vain for my old neighbors and seeing their once-crumbling houses transformed into expensive villas, until I began to feel like a ghost from a past long since cleaned up and carted off in truckloads of rubble.

One day, I was walking past as a man and a woman came out of my house. Inevitably, that was still the way I thought of it: my house. It had changed hands again since I had sold it, and I didn't know the new owners. They were well dressed — overdressed for Jerusalem. Through the open door, I glimpsed the clean sharp lines of an architect's renovation work. I hesitated, and then just as they were about to close the door behind them, went up and spoke to them.

"Excuse me, but . . . I used to live here." I waved my hand in a vague gesture of reassurance. "A long time ago.

But, well, I was just wondering if you wouldn't mind . . .
if I just looked inside a moment to see what it's like
now. . . ."

My voice trailed off as the two looked me up and down,
appraising me. I silently cursed my impetuosity. An oddly familiar feeling came over me, though I couldn't quite place it.
Their looks said, Who do you think you are to come intrud-
ing into our lives with tales of living in *our* house? What right
do you have to do this? It's our house, not yours.

Aloud, the woman said: "I don't see why. You wouldn't
recognize it at all. We had to do a lot of work on it." Ac-
cusation and pride mixed in her voice. She was American.

"I realize that," I said, feeling like a slum dweller trying
to talk to a millionaire, but persisting nonetheless. "I just
wanted to see what you've done with it. . . ."

The husband shrugged and looked questioningly at his wife.
"I don't see why not," he said.

She made a face. "I don't see why."

"Well, it can't do any harm."

"I suppose not," she replied ungraciously, and turned away.

As they were talking, I realized how I felt. It was like those
people who had come to various old houses in West Jerusalem just after the '67 war, timidly knocking, saying so politely, so gently, that they really didn't wish to disturb, but
you see, they used to live in this house, oh, long ago, before
'48. They were Arabs who had fled when the city was partitioned, gone to Jordanian-controlled territory and then found
themselves cut off from their property and their homes, which
had been declared abandoned property and let on ninety-nine-
year leases to Israeli citizens. They had come back now after
nineteen years. Just to see, just to look, just to remember how
it used to be.

And here, at the door of my house in Yemin Moshe, irrationally, I felt the same way. I, the Jew, a citizen of Israel who had spent most of her adult life in this place, felt like a Palestinian, dispossessed.

I walked into the house. "Just for one minute," the woman called after me. "We're in a hurry." And then in a loud aside to her husband: "You'd better go in with her, make sure . . ."

She was right: I wouldn't have recognized it. Ultramodern sofas instead of the beat-up old leather couch that was once there. An American-style bedroom set instead of the old brass bedstead. New red Mediterranean-type floor tiles instead of the battered Oriental-carpet tiles that I had taken such pride in. But above all, the walls, the lines. Where there had been separate rooms, there was now a huge open plan with a fake arched picture window. It had become the architect's dream of the perfect Jerusalem home. It was no longer mine.

✡

I told this story to Anton Shammas, hoping he'd give me a way to understand it. Anton is a poet, a novelist and a translator. His last book of poems — love poems — was *Shetach Hefker,* "No-Man's-Land."

His straight dark hair and regular features would make him handsome were it not for a faintly worried air about him — a particular tension, especially in the eyes, that seems to mark many Israeli Arab intellectuals. It is the look of the outsider, of the man who knows that whatever may happen, he can never feel quite at home in his own country.

In an ironic sense, the real Jews in Israel today are not Jews at all; they are Arabs.

Anton works on the divide between two languages, writing in Hebrew though his mother tongue is Arabic. "Sometimes

I feel that this is an act of cultural trespass, and the day may come when I shall have to account for it,'' he says. But meanwhile he speaks and writes some of the best Hebrew in the country today. That may be his own personal revenge, using the Jewish language better than the Jews themselves. Compliments on his style shower down on him. ''We have to try harder,'' he replies with a wry smile, perfectly aware that this is what Jews have said for centuries.

Like me, he grew up on a divide. He was an Arab in a Jewish educational system, I a Jew in a Catholic one. We were both determined by birth, time and place to lead divided lives. That is a productive situation for a writer, but a hard one for a person. He knows what I mean when I talk about the neglected beauty of Jerusalem before 1967. Divided people appreciate divided cities. We would both like to visit Berlin.

In his thirties now, and living in Jerusalem, Anton grew up in a small village in the Galilee, where his mother kept her books locked away in a closet. One day he found the key to the closet behind a mirror, unlocked it, and took out a Lebanese anthology of Arabic literature, a series of Hebrew reading primers, and an Egyptian translation of Willa Cather's novel *My Antonia*. It was the first novel he read.

A nine-year-old Arab boy in the Galilee devouring Cather's story of turn-of-the-century Bohemian homesteaders in Nebraska — at first it seems a cultural absurdity. But through Cather's sense of land and space, he discovered writing. And then there was the coincidence of the names — Anton, Antonia — irresistible to a young boy so eager to read that he risked punishment to do so. He became a writer, only to discover a painful anomaly.

Is he an Israeli writer, or an Israeli-Arab writer, or an Arab writer working in Hebrew? He considers himself an Israeli writer but finds the other two tags pinned on him instead. The saying in Israel is that when people abroad talk about Israelis, they mean Israeli Jews; that when Israeli Jews talk about Israelis, they mean Israeli Jews; and that when Israeli Arabs talk about Israelis, they too mean Israeli Jews. But the last is not necessarily so, and certainly not for Anton. When he talks about Israelis, he means all those who are Israeli citizens. And talking to him, I become aware of the distortion in my own thinking; built into my everyday language are the words *Israelis,* meaning Israeli Jews, and *Israeli Arabs,* meaning something other than simply Israeli.

It is an inevitable distortion in a country that defines itself as a Jewish state and guarantees automatic citizenship to any Jew who chooses to live here. In Anton's Israeli identity card, the word *Arab* is written under the heading Nationality. In mine, the word *Jewish.* Nationality and citizenship in the Jewish state are identical if you are a Jew, in conflict if you are an Arab. Though Anton was born here, and I only came here at age twenty, I can feel more at home here than he.

"An Israeli Arab you are, and an Israeli Arab you'll remain," he once wrote pessimistically, because to be an Arab in an Israel that is a Jewish state is an irresolvable paradox. He can conceive of an eventual solution for Palestinians on the West Bank, even if only in the far-off abstract. But so far as he can see, Palestinians inside Israel — Israeli Arabs — are in a dead-end situation.

"Only when the majority decide that the word *Israeli* will be written under Nationality in both my identity card and yours, only then will the vision of the next generation begin to be seen. But I personally believe that the Israeli Arabs are the eternal desert-dead, like the generation of Jews in Exodus who died in the desert. And that there is no solution to their problem. Not in this generation, and certainly not in the next. . . . They'll remain here as a millstone."

Many Israeli liberals cannot face that idea. They hope that when there is finally a Palestinian state — as it seems one day there will be, all the efforts of Menachem Begin, Gush Emunim and the messiah notwithstanding — the Israeli Arabs will move across the new border, relinquish their Israeli citizenship, and become Palestinian nationals. "Their idea is that I would leave here and go find another home in a Palestinian state," says Anton. "But that's not my solution, nor that of most other Israeli Arabs. We're not in exile. This is our home, right here in Israel. This is where we live."

Yet home *is* exile for him — an inner exile far deeper than the one the liberals talk about. This is his home, yet he cannot be at home here. Anton straddles the borders of language, culture and identity.

Such a man could act as a bridge between Arabs and Jews. His translations certainly do that. And in the early fifties, the liberal hope was that Israeli Arabs could bridge the gap. But Anton has become rather cynical about bridges lately. They get trampled on, he says.

✡

Amman, the capital of Jordan, would be just an hour's drive from Jerusalem if there were no border in between. In November of 1984, the Palestinian National Congress held its annual convention there. The congress inched closer to recognition of Israel than ever before, giving the go-ahead for a Palestinian-Jordanian plan for tripartite negotiations with the United States and Israel. At the same time, the Israeli Knesset was involved in an impassioned debate on whether the national flag should hang in the main hall of the parliament.

There was no flag in the hall because nobody had ever thought one necessary. But the ultranationalist Rafael Eytan, also known as Raful, who had been the army chief of staff in the first two years of the Lebanon war and was now intent on his political career as a Knesset member, considered this absence a national disgrace. He had called for a full debate, which now went on as though nothing else of any importance were happening — not the daily toll of the Lebanon war in its third year, not the spiraling deterioration of the economy as nightmare visions of 1,000-percent inflation came into being, and certainly not the existence of that convention just fifty miles away in Amman.

But Abd El-Wahab Darousha had taken note of the convention and decided that it was important that some contact be made. He too was a Member of Knesset; he was a Labor party representative, he was from Nazareth, and he was an Arab. He decided that he could forgo the debate on the flag. He boarded a plane for Cyprus, intending to change planes there and go on to Amman — a roundabout way to reach a city so close, but the only one available to an Israeli. Once there he planned to speak to the PNC convention and try to persuade it to accept Israel's basic demands for a negotiating position: no more terrorism, recognition of Israel's right to exist, recognition of United Nations Resolution 242, and abandonment of that part of the Palestinian Covenant that called for an end to ''the Zionist entity.''

He reached Cyprus, but there he got stuck. The Jordanians, smelling trouble when it was placed right under their noses, refused to give him a visa. By then, his plans had become public knowledge in Israel. And Darousha, a backbencher who had been so anonymous that no newspaper seemed able to spell his name right, became the scandal of the week.

An Israeli making contact with the enemy; worse still, a Member of Knesset; and even worse, an Arab. . . . Knesset members emerged from the debate on the flag to express shock, indignation, abhorrence. Right-wingers called for Darousha's parliamentary immunity to be lifted so that he could be prosecuted on his return (he would then be liable to fifteen years in prison for setting foot in an enemy country).

The flag debate was rapidly shelved for an emergency one on Darousha, who was still in Nicosia waiting in vain for a Jordanian visa. "Don't panic," liberal Yossi Sarid advised his fellow Knesset members with heavy irony, "he's not there yet. The worst has not yet happened. Don't lose heart."

Indeed, the Knesset panic was quite bewildering in its force. One could argue that Darousha was either a brave man or a naive one. The two are often the same. Whichever, admiration for his attempt seemed more appropriate than censure, and although ultranationalist extremists phoned in death threats to his family, most other Israelis seemed to agree with him. The Knesset may have thought that Darousha's plane flight was a threat to Israel's existence, but the famous "man on the street," as canvassed in news reports, clearly thought otherwise. "Why not?" people said with a shrug. "It's worth trying."

There were comparisons with popular restaurateur Abie Nathan's solo flight to Egypt in 1966 to persuade Nasser to make peace. (He had been politely received, though not by Nasser, and sent straight back.) There were also shades of Don Quixote up against the windmill. The Knesset had forgotten that Israelis, living in the shadow of the giant flails of the Middle East conflict, admired any attempt to charge it, however quixotic, so long as it was done with some sense of style and daring.

Darousha spoke to a *Ha'aretz* reporter by phone from Nicosia. "I am a son of the Palestinian people and I work in the service of my people," he said. "I am also a proud Israeli at the same time. My relation to the PNC is the same as that of Israeli Jews to French or American Jews. I want to help the members of the PNC advance their interests in peaceful ways.''

Clearly, Darousha thought he could be a bridge to peace.

That Friday, Anton Shammas expressed his and Darousha's disillusionment in his regular column in the Jerusalem paper *Kol Ha'Ir*. With an irony far stronger than usual for him, he wrote that Israeli Arabs had taken the idea of the bridge seriously. ''Liking bombastic images, they adopted it. It gave them a feeling that nevertheless they were wanted. They weren't particularly worried by the fact that bridges are anonymous structures, or that nobody pays much attention to them until they get to them, or that even then they just tread on them and continue onward. Most people don't even remember that there was a bridge at all. But the bridge, as a creation with developed self-respect, eternally declares its existence with a most praiseworthy masochism: 'Come tread on me! Tread on me!' And as in the well-known joke, the sadist answers with perverted pleasure: 'No!'

''Darousha was very hurt when he reached Cyprus and they stopped relating to him as a bridge. Nobody had ever heard of such a thing as a flying bridge, and nobody was surprised when he didn't get a visa. And nobody will bother to explain to Israeli Arabs that bridges are the first things to be destroyed in war — and in peace too.''

Bitter words from someone whose whole life is a bridge.

✡

Meanwhile I had my own problem with Darousha's dramatic flight. How could he have gone without arranging a visa beforehand? The question nagged me even while others came up with improvised explanations: he'd been promised a visa but hadn't realized how long it would take; he'd arranged the trip through the wrong people; he'd been too impetuous. No country takes kindly to people who turn up at its borders without the proper pieces of paper in hand. And I was particularly irked by Darousha's dilemma because I too had a visa problem. I had left the States without a visa to reenter.

"It's all right," the lawyer had said. "I'll just mail it to you when it comes through." But it hadn't come through. Instead, there had been a strange request from the U.S. Immigration and Naturalization Service for full records of my university studies. To get them from England was no problem. To get them right here in Jerusalem was. The university was on strike, and even when the strike was over, it would take weeks to compile my records, since I had studied before the Hebrew University went on computer.

I called the lawyer anxiously and heard the anxiety in his voice too. There was no way to talk to those responsible: the particular department processing the kind of visa I needed had retreated far up into New England, and its phone numbers were a closely guarded secret. No personal contact was possible. "I'm sure it will come through in the end," the lawyer said. "How long can the end take?" I asked. I had the strange experience of hearing a shrug over the transatlantic phone line.

My well-laid plans were now in limbo. A few weeks before, they had been clear enough: ten weeks in Jerusalem and then out, back to New York, to write recollections in the comparative tranquillity of that noisiest of cities. And if I couldn't go back? If my own bridge were burned by bureaucracy and took weeks or even months to rebuild?

At first I went through a stage of self-recrimination: I shouldn't have left without a definite reentry visa in my hand. But then if one waits for the world of visas before acting, caution overtakes action and the time to move passes. Then came a stage of panic. Suddenly the most important thing of all was to get out of Jerusalem, to get back to New York, to continue exactly as planned. I was terrified lest Jerusalem claim me again, pull me back into it despite my protests. And indeed it was beginning to do that, because then came a third stage. Slowly, like long arms stretching comfortably in the midmorning sun, came the increasingly seductive idea that I could just stay on here as long as was necessary.

I had constructed my own bridge, linking Jerusalem and New York and London, but it was at the Jerusalem end that I felt most comfortable. I had never realized this before, and the new knowledge surprised me. I had not yet reached that point where the politics becomes so oppressive that all you want to do is escape: *Ruh min hon.*

XIII

A<small>N</small> old saying has it that when you put two stones together in this country, they grow into a wall.

That is what you do in a stony country: you gather the stones and make them into walls. You live inside the stone. You live with it. You become an expert on stone.

Herman Melville, sharp-eyed, saw this when he traveled here, and he remembered all the stones in the Bible, where "monuments and memorials are set up of stones; men are stoned to death; the figurative seed falls in stony places." The Judean hills are "one accumulation of stones: stony mountains and stony plains, stony torrents and stony roads, stony walls and stony fields, stony houses and stony tombs, stony eyes and stony hearts."

Stony hearts. I still have the pharaoh's heart that Dan once gave me — a museum reproduction of the exquisitely carved stone heart that was placed on the breast of the mummy before burial, so that he would not go into the next world without a heart. On one side the goddess Hathor smiles catlike from the stone; on the other, the pharaoh, lionlike, tramples his enemies beneath his feet.

There are no pharaohs anymore, but there are people with that blind pharaonic ambition: the Arik Sharons and the obsessed messianists, whose hearts still turn to stone. There are always such people, everywhere in the world. I prefer those whose hearts are cut and bruised by all this stone. The harshness makes the heart vulnerable. It divides, heals, and divides again, continually aching — a heart condition that develops slowly, the longer you live here, and never goes away. For some it worsens, and the heart breaks.

Heartbreak, then. I think of the strange series of postcards sold "in all fine stores" in town. They are variations on the design of the Israeli flag, the two broad bands of blue against a white background with a blue Star of David in the middle. They were printed as a nationalist gesture, but the play on the familiar symbols is contorted in some of them into what sometimes seems a horribly apt surrealism. In one, the bands have become ribbons, tied up in knots around the star. In another, the whole flag is marked off as a jigsaw puzzle, but in the center, where the star should be, there is just the black gap of a missing piece. And in a third, the star remains intact but the blue bands have narrowed into thin jagged lines like those of an electrocardiogram reading — a bad one, with mayhem above and below the star. Panic stations. The heart out of control. Heart attack.

I left Jerusalem in 1979 as Dan was recovering from a heart attack. It had been a severe one, but after so many wars and so many injuries, it would take more than that to kill him. Yet his heart was clearly weakening under the constant assault of reality, the burden of any journalist who cares.

We had become close over the years, the friendship formed around long discussions on slow sunny afternoons, when the sun filtered through the willow tree outside into his huge hall-like living room and played on the ornate tile patterns of the floor to make marbled carpets of light. It was an old thick-walled house, facing the single-track railway line that brings two trains a day up through the hills to Jerusalem, pulling in sedately and gently, often with no passengers aside from the driver and guard. In any other country, this would be a very tranquil house.

Sometimes our discussions would turn into arguments — about journalism, terrorism, nuclear war, morality. He had the certainty of experience, of having seen too much. And the blindness of it too. He was the old kind of Israeli, steeped in the idealism that had shaped his commitment to the country. I was another kind, another generation, either more cynical or more realistic. I had been as upset as he when Begin was elected in 1977, but less surprised. I had seen the trend to the right among younger Israelis as the fact of being an occupying power drilled deep into their minds, distorting the old values and making the unacceptable acceptable. I had thought it could be staved off for a while yet, at least for another few years. That had been my blindness, my wishful thinking: "Not yet." But the appointment at Samarra was kept.

There had been one afternoon, a few months before Dan's heart attack, when we had argued about good and evil. The limits of both were very clear to him, but for me they lay in a haze of complexity. "It's easier for you," I said (I must have been losing the argument), "because you came out of a simpler, clearer world. I was born a month after Hiroshima, into a far more complex one. Beside that, everything seems relative."

"It was never that clear," he replied. His eyes narrowed in focus on the past. "No, it never was. It just looks that way from a distance. There never was a time of innocence."

I hesitated. Then: "I wonder will all this seem simple from a distance too, if in forty years' time people will sit here in this house and look back on this year and wonder at how clear all the issues were then. Will they call us innocent as I called your generation innocent? What will be the breaking point for them, the event that takes them one more step away? It's always a war, somehow. For you it was World War II. For me it was the '67 war. But how many wars does it take until this loss of innocence turns us into stone? Until this whole country becomes like Lot's wife, eternally looking back, incapable of looking forward?''

More rhetorical questions. By then we both feared the same thing.

The next war — the Lebanon war — was the war of our fears. Dan called on the second day, wanting to know what I'd heard about it in New York through reports from Beirut. ''I'm not sure what's going on,'' he said, ''but the official line that we're going in only forty kilometers doesn't make sense, not for the size of the operation.'' He'd just had a fight with his editors over the battle for the Beaufort Castle the night before. He argued that it was not a significant battle and that the real news was the whole strategy of the campaign; they wanted a full account of the battle. The argument ended with his slamming down the phone and writing the piece he would have written in any case.

Dan was right, but that was little consolation either at the time or a year later, when I'd read the account of the Beaufort battle in the Ze'ev Schiff and Ehud Ya'ari book *Israel's Lebanon War,* and been stunned by it, as though I were discovering for the first time, all over again, the sheer destructive absurdity of warfare.

It was a needless battle for a worthless objective. The ruined Crusader fortress was a PLO stronghold on top of the most commanding mountain in the region, true, but by the time a commando unit was assigned to take it, the main thrust of the Israeli assault had gone on northward, overtaking Beaufort, so that, according to Schiff and Ya'ari, actual developments in the field ''dictated that an assault should be avoided altogether, or at least postponed, because it might well prove unnecessary." In fact, an order was given to cancel the attack, but it never reached the commander of the unit concerned, a political dove named Guni Harnik. The canceling order was "simply swallowed up, misplaced or forgotten somewhere down the line."

Twenty-three of them carried out the assault. Motti Goldman, the second in command, said later that "we fought to take the flag away from them." A lot of deaths for a piece of linen.

They fought at night. Schiff and Ya'ari described the battle in detail. "They had to cover 150 meters with enemy positions all along their left flank. All Motti could see were the flashes of fire coming from three or four positions on his left. He didn't know what was happening behind him, and when he dived down beside Guni and turned back to glance at his men, he was dismayed to see that only ten of them remained."

Only eight got up to begin the second stage of the assault. "Motti was sure he wouldn't get very far, that any second now a burst of gunfire would put an end to the whole grotesque scene. The battle struck him as a surrealistic dream played out in a deafening racket. As he ran along the edge of the trench, he could see his silhouette flickering on the fortress wall like the dance of a crazed giant. He shot a Palestinian who was scurrying through the trench firing and shouting incomprehensibly. Then two Israeli soldiers came up from behind and offered Motti additional grenades. Right afterward, Guni arrived.

"Together Motti Goldman and Guni Harnik stood facing a long concrete position that contained a single Palestinian fighter spraying the area with occasional fire. The Israelis did not call on him to surrender, and he showed no signs of giving himself up in order to save his life. Two Israeli fighters — Motti Goldman, a self-proclaimed hawk, and Guni Harnik, a man who called for compromise with the Palestinians — stood side by side in a trench at a ruined Crusader castle in Lebanon opposite a lone trapped Palestinian, sharing a single choice: kill or be killed. As one man lobbed grenades at the concrete position, the other pumped out bursts of gunfire. Some twenty grenades had been futilely expended on the position when Guni suddenly jerked backward and let out a short moan as his head fell limply forward. A few minutes later he was dead, a bullet embedded in his chest. The Palestinian continued to fire until Motti, in a mixture of terror and anger, hurled a huge explosive charge at the concrete position and blew it to bits.''

The battle was over.

The next day, Menachem Begin and Arik Sharon flew in by helicopter to pose for the press at Beaufort, ''self-congratulatory and slightly ludicrous figures,'' as Schiff and Ya'ari described them. The ultimate insult came when Sharon, then defense minister, boasted that no Israelis had been killed taking the position. ''A junior lieutenant from the commando unit left to man the fortress was so rattled by the carefree mood of the visit that he suddenly blurted out: 'What are you talking about? Six of my friends were killed here!' Sharon seemed dazed by the statement.''

Begin and Sharon were quickly whisked off the mountaintop. Begin went back to Jerusalem and never set foot on Lebanese soil again. Two years later, he'd fall into deep depression, and then into a hermitlike life of silence. Sharon went on to Beirut. A few months later he'd be charged with indirect responsibility for the Sabra and Shatila massacre of Palestinians by Phalangists and be forced to resign as defense minister — only to become trade and industry minister in the next Israeli government.

I was in Jerusalem shortly after Sabra and Shatila, just as the Kahan Supreme Court Commission began its inquiry into what had happened in the two Palestinian refugee camps on the outskirts of Beirut. The day Menachem Begin testified, it rained. Black clouds ranged over Jerusalem. Winter curled icy fingers up into the mountains.

Bill Farrell came through from Beirut. He had been the *New York Times* correspondent in Jerusalem for some years, and then in Cairo, and then in Beirut. While Tom Friedman concentrated on the hard news, eventually winning a Pulitzer Prize for his coverage of Sabra and Shatila, Bill roamed the streets of Beirut during that summer's siege, through a city without electricity and water for days at a time.

"A City of Murdered Sleep" ran the headline on one of his dispatches. Reading them, I saw Bill help pull the remains of his assistant's family from an apartment house reduced to ruins by Israeli bombing. I watched with him as a young boy danced with the rats around a smouldering pile of rubble. I saw the newly homeless sitting in stunned silence in the sweltering streets, and an old man squatting on his heels and looking blankly into the distance as the planes came in yet again. The old man's right hand was held high, and from it dangled a clear plastic bag half full of water. A goldfish swam in the water. And there was a hole in the bottom of the bag, so that the water dripped slowly into the dust.

That old man haunted Bill's dreams in the moments when he fell into a fitful sleep. Surrounded by too much horror, the mind latches onto some absurdity instead. For me it was storks being machine-gunned down in midmigration. For Bill it was an old man watching his goldfish die.

I hardly recognized him when he opened the door to his room in the American Colony Hotel. Whatever words I was about to say stuck in my throat. "Are you ill?" I said instead. He had never been fleshy, but I had also never seen him as gaunt as this, with deep black circles around his eyes. He looked as though he had just walked out of a concentration camp. Or as though he had cancer. (Two years later, I would curse even having thought that: they discovered a cancer the size of a grapefruit in his left lung and he was dead within months — the best and the brightest.)

Bill's job, like Dan's, was that of the observer. But it is hard to be just an observer here. Impossible, perhaps. The Middle East has long tentacles, and they reach deep inside you like those winter winds reaching into Jerusalem. They reach into your mind and your heart and your guts and hold fast there as though with barbed tips, twisting and turning and never letting go. Only the most innocent, the most blithe or the most stupid can remain uninvolved.

I went over some of the Kahan Commission testimony together with Dan: the anxious phone calls from men at the post closest to the camps through to headquarters, the messages left for ministers and never answered, the growing realization that "something was happening" — all of which was "simply swallowed up, misplaced or forgotten somewhere down the line" until two months later it was regurgitated, found and remembered under the probing of Israel's Supreme Court judges.

The Phalangists who had committed the massacre had been Israel's allies. Strange allies for a Jewish state. They were formed in the 1930s on the model of the Italian fascists. They went into Sabra and Shatila with Israeli encouragement and cooperation. In fact, many Israelis believed that Arik Sharon had intended for there to be a massacre, thinking that this would cause panic among the Palestinians and make them flee to Syria. Some even agreed with this as a strategy. Then there were those who argued that the whole affair had nothing to do with them. Menachem Begin's statement that "goys kill goys and they blame the Jews" was the crudest expression of this position. But there were also many who found it hard to believe that Israeli forces could think a massacre was going on under their noses and do nothing to stop it. They turned out for the largest demonstration ever held in Israel. Four hundred thousand people — 10 percent of the country's population — crowded the main square of Tel Aviv to pressure Begin into setting up the commission of inquiry.

The commission's report seemed like a resurrection of Israel's old values. But its recommendations were followed only in letter, not in spirit. Arik Sharon was removed as defense minister, but remained in the cabinet. Menachem Begin did not resign, as many thought he surely must. In the government, it was business as usual. But not in the country.

The massacre had crushed Dan in a way that his heart attacks could not. He sat crumpled in his chair as we went through the commission's testimony, his usual straight posture broken. "The question is not whether anyone imagined there would be a massacre," he said bitterly, "but whether there was anyone there who imagined there would *not* be one." His eyes narrowed with pain at the thought. I had never seen him this despairing before.

There is a phrase in Israel that is often repeated in bad times, when another of the best and the brightest is killed or a new scandal breaks open someone's life. It is what Joshua's spies said to him when they came back from a scouting trip into Israel: *eretz ochelet yoshveiha*, "a land that devours its inhabitants." (Two and a half years after the Kahan Commission, Israeli tank crews finally coming back to Israel from Lebanon would display large signs on their tanks with a bitter play on those words: *Lebanon — eretz ochelet covsheiha*, "a land that devours its conquerors.")

Dan too had been devoured. He had stayed in one place while the country went rushing past him in another direction, one he never dreamed of, not for Israel. He had discovered that this country can break your heart with dreams betrayed.

Betrayal is a highly charged word in a country so attuned to security. And while Arik Sharon accused those who opposed him of betraying their country, clearly convinced that *l'état c'est moi,* there were many who felt that their country had betrayed them. Then there were others, like Dan, who felt they themselves had been guilty of another kind of betrayal.

His whole face creased in self-recrimination as he talked: he hadn't done enough for the country, he could have done far more, he should have been more active. "If only . . ." he kept saying. If only he had entered politics instead of staying on the journalistic sidelines, if only he had spoken out directly instead of trying to maintain an almost impossible objectivity, if only he had campaigned instead of reported. . . .

I couldn't bear to see him like this. My own inability to listen led me into a cruel retort, as though violent words could wipe out the pain from that crumpled face: "Why, do you think you're the messiah? Do you think you could have saved the country? The seeds of all this were sown long ago, and we all knew that and did nothing about it. What difference would it have made what you'd have done?"

Yet I knew the lie the moment I said it. It would have made a difference — the difference of having fought instead of just complaining about what was happening, and the difference of struggling against the despair that comes with the sense of the inevitable. Dan's bitterness was the blackest of all. It was that of someone who knew how to fight but had not thought it necessary. And now he felt too old to do it.

But then, was his inaction any worse than my own? I had seen what was happening clearly enough, but instead of staying and fighting it, I had left in exhaustion. I began to wonder if any of us ever do the right things at the right time, or if we just spend most of our lives persuading ourselves that we did. As I spoke, the plaintive whistle of the afternoon train sounded from far down the valley.

"Can't we talk about something else for a while?" Dan pleaded suddenly. "We used to talk about so much. And now all I ever seem to talk about is politics." With a shock, I saw tears in his eyes. Answering tears came to mine, and I swallowed to keep them back, remembering that this is a place that can teach you how to cry: tears for the dead and tears for the living, tears for peace and tears for war, tears of laughter and tears of joy, and then the slow deep tears of helplessness clawing at your soul.

Sometimes it seems as though the whole country is one huge Wailing Wall. Only the turtledoves are above it, looking down on all these tears. And the hawks, circling above them, waiting.

XIV

"**L**ISTEN," said Udi, his deep bass voice testing the capacity of the telephone wires. "I've got these two visitors in town from New Zealand —"

New Zealand? Here in Jerusalem? It was early in the morning, but I was suddenly wide awake.

"— and they want to go out into the Judean desert. Want to join us?"

Twenty minutes later I was clambering into Udi's jeep.

I hadn't been to the desert since that day of the first rain, and it was time to get out and "clean the head," as the Hebrew phrase goes — to escape the thickening clouds of politics, if only for a day. The fact that Marilyn and Peter were from New Zealand gave an extra fillip to my anticipation of tranquillity.

Their looks, like their names, were reminders of how far they had traveled. They were both blond, pale, and in their early thirties. They also knew a good guide when they saw one: Udi had founded an adventure-travel company some years before. He was a desert person, more at home in the wild than in town and frustrated by how little he got out into the open now that the firm had grown and he was trapped behind a desk playing administrator. His restlessness had increased since his jail term some months before. He was a member of

Yesh Gvul ("There's a Limit," or, in a deliberate play on words, "There's a Border"), a group of reserve army officers who refused to serve in Lebanon and went to jail for that refusal. "It was worth it," he said. "There was nothing to do in jail but play backgammon and smoke. So I got very good at backgammon, and I stopped smoking."

Marilyn and Peter were fascinated by the very idea of the desert, as was I by the idea of New Zealand, and they chattered excitedly for a while. But as Udi drove headlong down the winding road, they fell into a tight-lipped silence. Perhaps they had heard that more Israelis had been killed on the roads than in all the wars together. I hung on to my seat, wondering how it was that a gentle man like Udi should become so fierce behind the wheel.

We passed through Bethlehem to pick up long finger bread and *zaatar* spice, felafel, nuts and apples, and then set off along the mountain ridge southward, on the Hebron road. I didn't ask if there was a gun in the jeep; I didn't want to know. Soon we'd be turning off the road into the desert in any case.

The turn was just past a collection of stark housing cubes crowded behind a ring of barbed wire: the Gush Emunim settlement of Tekoa. We set off east on a dirt track, and Udi slowed down. He had no choice. Soon we were driving along a wadi bed, the jeep careening up and down over the stones like a boat tossing on a rough sea. Within minutes, the desert dust was in our eyes and noses, mouths and hair.

Large parts of the wide wadi had been churned up, and huge tractor tracks scarred the landscape. Another settlement to be built, out here in the desert? Udi shook his head: "Armored corps maneuvers. We're in the middle of a training ground. The only day you can come here is today, Shabbat. Every other day they're firing." Even the army keeps Shabbat.

The farther into the desert we drove, the rougher the going

became. I was getting impatient with driving, and wanted to get out and walk. Udi stopped the jeep. "Over there," he said, nodding toward the rock hillside about half a mile away. I peered, and made out a flock of black goats gathered at the foot of the incline. There might be water there.

Drawn on by the sound of goat bells on the wind, we walked on over. Sure enough, there was a Bedouin well: just a hole in the rock, its sides scored with the marks of centuries of ropes. The shepherd was bent low over it, hauling up bucket after bucket. He splashed the water into a dip in the rock and the goats lined up to drink, waiting their turn according to the flock's own rules of precedence. The shepherd glanced up, readjusted his keffiyas, greeted us, and bent back to his work. Just watching him hurt my back.

A couple of goats brayed at our arrival, and a couple more moved aside slightly to let us pass. The lead goat, its sides swollen with water, stood on a nearby ledge. A string of huge golden-orange amber beads hung round its neck; they would have fetched a hundred dollars from a tourist in the Old City. I scrambled up onto the ledge (the goat shifted a leg to acknowledge my presence), leaned back against the rock wall, half in the sun and half in the shade, and felt the tensions draining out of me into this desert starkness. I was covered in dust, yet I felt clean, freed of care. It was good to be back in the desert.

Marilyn and Peter were photographing the Bedouin and his flock. I looked down at them, trying to compare their high mountain lakes to this field of rock and dust. The physical landscape was so different, but the essence of it was probably the same — the same peacefulness, the same silence, the same haunting sense of beauty. If you could forget the politics, that is. But you couldn't, not here; the whole route we'd taken had shown us that.

The shepherd finished watering the flock, took a drink himself, and set off across the hills. He had to be out of here before sundown, when the firing would start again. Yet the only reason there'd been water in this well so late in the season had been because this *was* a firing range, and access was limited. Most of the other wells in the desert were dry.

We stayed on and ate the supplies we'd picked up in Bethlehem. Marilyn clambered up behind me, bringing me a canteen of water from the well. It was sharp with minerals, but cool. We sat silently side by side for a while, and then she sighed. "I envy you this desert," she said. "It's spare and basic. There's nothing to distract you here. It's very pure."

I smiled. It seemed an ironic twist on the old saying that the grass is always greener on the other side. "You know we envy you the peace and beauty of all that greenery in New Zealand."

"Oh, I know, it's beautiful there all right, especially South Island. But nothing ever happens there. It's as though it has no past. Whereas here, with all the wars . . ."

"Here we've got too much past."

She hesitated a moment, then said, "You were in Jerusalem in the 1967 war, weren't you? And the Yom Kippur War too. You saw those wars." Her tone was almost one of awe. I nodded and said nothing, embarrassed. Udi had been in the front line in both those wars, and fighting through any war is immeasurably harder than just living through it. But then it may be easier for an outsider to grasp the role of a spectator in war than that of a soldier. That may be one of the effects of television, which brings the sight of battle into everyone's living room — from a safe distance — but not the smell of fear and burned flesh.

I had a sudden flash of pure absurdity. Here I was feeling utterly peaceful in the middle of a firing range, sitting beside someone from the Israeli dream of a peaceful country who seemed to envy us the experience of war. I had heard Marilyn's awe and envy in other people's voices, in other countries. It was as though living through a war were an experience that made me somehow special, setting me apart as though I had some knowledge of the meaning of life and death that they could never attain.

But I do not think that knowledge an enviable one, even if it exists. If it does exist, then the whole country has it. And most people here would far prefer to be without it.

The incongruity of the scene deepened as my thoughts wandered to New York, to a minor ritual that has been established between myself and a certain editor over the past few years. Every now and again, he calls and asks me to lunch. We eat well, drink a little, and then when he suspects that the moment is right, he abruptly steers the conversation to the same question: "When are you going to write a book about war and peace?"

The first time he asked it, I burst out laughing, breaking the hushed murmur of business deals being made at tables around us. I reached for the Perrier water and said: "You have to be kidding." Laughter still bubbling inside me along with the Perrier, I pointed out that Tolstoy had already written that book, and that so far as I was concerned, his *War and Peace* was unsurpassable. But to an ambitious New York editor, that was no deterrent. Garnering my defenses, I argued that having existed through three wars and one peace did not make me an expert. Each year I'd say the same thing, and each following year he'd make the same proposal, until I finally realized that in his eyes I really was an expert on war and peace.

At first I thought it a peculiarly American reaction. American wars have been fought far from home, and despite Vietnam, the glorification of war still goes on, as much in apparently antiwar movies as in the openly patriotic type made after World War II and recently enjoying a revival in the gleaming muscles of Rambo and company. But I soon saw that this admiration and awe was not limited to the United States; it was the reaction of people from countries living in relative peace. And because I was a journalist, I found that much of it was focused on me.

Movies with war-correspondent heroes have become very popular in the past few years. Foreigners run around against the exotic background of somebody else's war in search of some arcane and imaginary truth about life and death (and only incidentally, it seems, in search of news). Often they find love along the way, or at least sex, and the big scene is played against the swelling strains of gunfire or under the apparently stimulating threat of imminent arrest or death. Whether it is Asia or the Middle East or Central America, the "natives" are always the ones to get killed; the journalists themselves survive to moralize about the existential dilemma of mankind.

For a time, such movies were coming so thick and fast that it seemed if you just combined the word *journalist* with the words *war zone* you had a contemporary formula for romance.

There are plenty of journalists who subscribe to this formula themselves. They tend to be the ones who have not spent much time in a war zone. They may have read Hemingway at too early and too impressionable an age, and taken his image of tough romanticism too literally. Or the formula may simply be a means of gaining self-importance in what is, after all, the quintessential occupation of the outsider. And so they welcome that sudden gleam of wondering respect that I heard again in Marilyn's voice that day in the desert, and willingly fill in the expectant silence as the questioner waits for war stories.

But to anyone who has heard too many war stories, there is no thrill left in them. There is only a haunting and ever-increasing sense of waste.

Knowing war is nothing to be proud of. If anything, I am ashamed of it. Partly that shame is for a knowledge I would much rather not have — too intimate an acquaintance with darkness. Wars were easier by far when I was a schoolgirl, learning the dates of battles with the same bored aloofness I brought to bear on the rules of grammar. History was a matter of exams, not people. Until that afternoon in 1967 when I saw the faces of those who had been fighting in the Old City, I had no real sense of what happened to people in war.

I also suffer the shame of those who can only watch, worry and mourn, fated by age or sex or bad eyesight or flat feet to let others fight instead, and to look in their eyes when they come back — if they come back — and see there an awareness of mortality that most of us spend our lifetimes trying to suppress. In the act of killing, as I knew from friends who had fought hand to hand, you see with awful clarity how fragile life can be.

There are too many others in Israel who know far more about war than I ever want to know. It makes them no better and no worse than they are capable of becoming. Some it coarsens; they are the ones who boast of how many they have killed. After Lebanon, there are few of those left, except among noncombatants. Others it makes more human. One friend sent a postcard from the front during the Yom Kippur War. Like all army mail, it was sent from "somewhere in Israel." He described field flowers he had found, ones he'd never seen before. "I'll tell you what it's like here when I get back," he wrote. The postcard arrived after the news of his death.

But most soldiers draw a line between what happened in war and the rest of their lives. They consign battle to a confined space at the back of awareness. Some grind their teeth at night, and some talk or cry out in their sleep, but by day they live normally enough. It is hard to carry around the memory of the fear and smells of battle; they have to be repressed to make everyday life possible.

What continually surprises me, however, is that nobody asks with that same tone of awe and respect if I was in Jerusalem in November 1977, when Egyptian president Anwar Sadat made his dramatic visit. With so much awareness of war, it is easy to lose the memory of peace. Because there was also peace. And I am inordinately proud of having known that, as though just by being there at the time I had somehow helped make it happen.

For the forty hours of that visit, the shame of war in me was purged by the vision of peace. And that was something I was happy to tell this New Zealander about, as we sat in the shade of a rock ledge in the middle of a desert firing range.

XV

By late October of 1977, winter had begun to chill the Jerusalem nights. We turned on the heaters to warm the walls for an hour or two after dark, though the days were still hot, sometimes almost balmy. I have forgotten just who was on strike at the time. I think it was the teachers, airport ground crews and telephone repairmen, with the engineers and nurses also threatening action. It was one of those times when the whole country seemed capable of sliding gradually to a halt, with everyone holding everyone else hostage to their demands.

I was working on an economics article. I'd written the story too many times before. The quotes were horribly familiar, with the same dire predictions of imminent collapse. Only the figures changed: the rate of inflation, the value of the dollar against the local currency, and the size of the deficit kept on rising. Every time I reported on the economic situation, it seemed as bad it could get — until it got worse. Resentful of the blue sky outside, I worked slowly. The phone rang.

"Did you hear?" It was Dan.

"Hear what?" I was smiling already, having caught the bantering tone in his voice. Dan's stories were often just tall enough to tease the fine line between my cynicism and my credulity.

"That Sadat is flying to Jerusalem to talk to all one hundred and twenty Members of Knesset."

"Right. And Arafat's flying to the moon that day."

"You don't believe me? Listen to the news at eleven."

I was intrigued. "So what's really going to be on the news at eleven?"

"You'll see. It's true. At least that's what Sadat has just announced to the Egyptian parliament. Listen to the news and we'll talk later. Work well."

"Sure," I said.

Very soon, I'd be saying "for sure" instead. Those two English words — Anwar Sadat's pet phrase — were to become an integral part of the Hebrew language for the next two years.

It took days for Begin to call Sadat on his word, and even then the invitation to Jerusalem was issued with what seemed a jaded assumption that it would be ignored. But then suddenly there was a date. Even a time. And for the next two weeks, a quiet refrain of unreality sounded beneath the comings and goings of everyday life. Sadat was coming to Jerusalem. The enemy was coming. To talk. To make peace. It was impossible, yet it was going to happen. Like everyone else, I veered between belief and disbelief.

"Is it real?" I asked Dan.

"We'll see on November nineteenth," he replied. What else could he say? And how could we believe it?

Peace means very little to those who have always lived in peace. They take it for granted. It is the normal way of things for them. But to those for whom war had become the normal way of things, peace was a golden ideal. It shimmered in the distance like a mirage. It glowed in a childlike vision of Egyptians and Israelis falling into each other's arms, hugging and crying, calling each other Brother, Sister, Friend. . . .

Of course we knew that wouldn't happen, but we didn't know what would.

When we tried to imagine Sadat standing on the podium of the Knesset, we saw the past instead: hysterical crowds in the streets of Cairo calling for the Jews to be pushed into the sea before the Six Days War, and phalanxes of Egyptian soldiers swarming up the east bank of the Suez Canal in the Yom Kippur War, taking the supposedly impregnable Bar-Lev Line by surprise. Old images of war blocked the new ones of peace. We could only wait and see.

The streets were empty that Saturday evening. Everyone was in front of a television set. At Ilana and David's we sat tense with waiting. On the screen, politicians, diplomats and religious dignitaries milled around on the tarmac of Lod airport, guarded by what seemed to be a whole brigade of heavily armed paratroopers, half visible in the shadows of the arc lights. All of Israel's leadership was there. The minutes passed. The guest was late. The studiedly casual conversation began to wear thin, and the cameras picked up the forced smiles of anxiety. The politicians started to look uncomfortable, almost lost, unsure of what script to follow. They might have been extras in a surrealist French movie, waiting for the director to fly in and decide how this scene should run.

The two television commentators were just as edgy. Every now and again, one of them would say, "Listen!" and there was a silence as both tried to hear the sound of an approaching plane. All other traffic in and out of the airport had been canceled. But then the other would say, "No, that's not it," and the two would fall back on the desperate small talk of time filling.

And then even we at home could hear the drone of the plane. The camera searched the darkness, but was blinded by the airport lights. There was just the sound of a plane coming in

169

for landing. We strained toward the screen, as other people had strained to see other night planes arriving, in other times and in other countries — ragged bands of refugees, resistance fighters waiting for a drop, civilians waiting for an air raid. . . . Like children watching a suspense movie, we didn't dare speak.

"It's landed," the commentators said. "It's taxiing in . . ."

And still the cameras were blind.

And then "Here it is," whispered Ilana, and the plane wheeled into the light. It seemed to take forever to slow down, a small eternity to stop. Finally the engines were cut, and they whined down into silence. Everyone on the tarmac stood as though frozen, staring, just as we were.

Someone barked an order. A crew came running. A staircase moved to the plane. A red carpet was rolled out from the bottom step of the stairs. And then after that flurry of activity, everything was silent again. Nothing moved.

My eyes narrowed in absolute focus on that airplane door, as though if I looked hard enough I could penetrate the metal and see what was inside. I made unspoken bets with myself — the same bets Ilana and David were making, with the same odds calculated by every commando officer on that tarmac. Maybe it was all a bluff. Maybe a unit of Egyptian paratroopers would fan out with guns blazing the minute the door opened and shoot down the whole of Israel's leadership. Or there'd be a bomb timed to go off any moment. Or the airplane door would swing open to reveal . . . nothing, an empty plane, a blank cruel joke on a people who had allowed themselves to hope despite themselves.

And then there he was.

The impossible was happening.

Alone, he walked down the staircase. "He" — the only person meant those days when anyone in Israel said "he," as though he were the messiah. Still staring as though my life depended on it, I saw the light glint off his cheekbones, heard the swelling roar of applause and cheering, felt the tears well up in my eyes as he stepped onto the red carpet and — "Oh my God" — embraced Menachem Begin. Camera flashes sliced through the air, cutting the scene into a series of stills, and as he straightened from that embrace, the Israeli army band began to play the Egyptian national anthem. It was music I had never heard before, and I tasted salt as the tears spilled over and I shook my head in ecstatic disbelief.

Suddenly we were all hugging and crying and laughing, still staring at the screen even as we embraced, unable to take our eyes away from it. Brandy glasses were suddenly full, everyone was talking, and all the questions that would come up later were drowned for the moment in the conviction that this was still the land of miracles, where the impossible could happen.

And then, as we refilled the glasses, came the bitterness at the realization of how easy it was, once it was done. "Why couldn't it have been done before?" was the question. And another one, growled in resentment: "Why Begin? After all these years, Begin is the one he embraces. . . ." We knew the irony that the seemingly intransigent right is in a stronger position to make peace moves; we had the example of President Nixon opening relations with China. And we knew that it is naive to expect history to be fair; what you dream of can indeed happen, but with that cruel twist, that fickle finger of fate that now pointed to the most unlikely of Israel's leaders as the man to make peace. We knew the answers, but we still couldn't help asking the questions.

For the next forty hours, Jerusalem was strangely quiet, folded in on itself in intense concentration. Everyone focused on the olive skin that seemed so tanned and healthy next to

Begin's pasty paleness, on the confident smile of a man who had risked his life for history — and at least for the space of these days, had won. We kept by the television screens, hanging on his every movement, word, gesture and smile as though they contained the answers to all our questions. The only time there was anyone in the streets was when he drove from one place to another — to the Holocaust memorial of Yad Vashem, to El-Aqsa, the third-holiest mosque in Islam, to the Knesset, where he spoke to the whole nation.

"No more war," he said. And those three words made the flesh real.

People began to ask a new question: "Do you think he means it?" It was the question of a people wary of being trapped by hope, and just as wary of being bound into despair. Those who dared, found a heady joy in those days. Freed from the messy particularities of their everyday lives, they breathed the rarefied air of a mythic Jerusalem — *Ir Shalem,* the city of peace.

✡

The end of war. At first it sounds like the end of pain — a relief, an ending, no more. And yet the euphoria when it happens! Every cell of your body comes alive with hope. You endured war, and learned to accept the dull leaden burden of it. But now hope rushes through you like a sudden winter rain in the desert.

Within a few hours of a desert downpour, flowers bloom in colors and shapes not even found in the field guides, so rare is the rain that makes them appear. But the ground is parched by so much dryness. The water doesn't sink in; it runs off. It sweeps on down into the nearest ravine, gathering force as it turns into a flash flood, a roar of boulders and mud and spray tumbling in a destructive rush to its own exhaustion at the ravine's end. It is a matter of hours, even minutes — a short-lived drama. The rare desert flowers shrivel and die within a few days. Only the seeds live on, shrunk into a state of suspended life, waiting with inhuman patience for the next rain, however long it may take to come.

Ten months passed. No peace was born. The miracle faded into illusion, giddy hope into familiar despair.

Bo'az went into the army that year. Like Ilana, I was astonished that he was suddenly old enough. He came home on his first leave with hair shorn close to his skull, a heavy tan, and the gaunt look of someone who's been on maneuvers. He seemed years older than he had been a month before.

He'd collected stones while he was out in the field, stopping to cram his pockets with them and weighing himself down still further on forced marches under a ninety-pound pack and weapons. He laid them out on the kitchen table: flint worked thousands of years ago into arrowheads and scraping tools, smooth gold and pink eggs of quartz, fragments of geodes with inner crystals sparkling purple and silver in the light, green lines of copper tracing through red granite. The stones told us he'd been in the Sinai, training to fight yet another war there if need be.

He slept right through that first leave. "That's my baby inside all that khaki," Ilana insisted. "If only he'd never have to fight. . . ." Peace had disappeared from our horizon, though Lebanon was still a distant country.

Bo'az finished his paratroop training and then promptly transferred to the far less prestigious armored corps over the protests of his officers, who wanted him to train as a paratroop officer himself. "I don't like the atmosphere in the paratroops," was all he'd say. "Too elite." Ilana worried. There was good reason to avoid the tank corps if you could, and that was the prospect of being caught in a red-hot shell of steel with no exit except to leap through the flames and then roll in agony on the ground, trying to put out the fire on your flesh. "Don't worry," said Bo'az, "I'm doing the commander's course. I'll be in the turret." I couldn't imagine his face under the helmet, earphones and mouthpiece of a tank commander, probably because I feared the image of his head and shoulders exposed in the turret, vulnerable to the first bullet.

Like Bo'az, I spent much of that time in the Sinai, but not in the army. While the politicians bickered over this desert, I wandered through it, making it my own. I got lost, got dehydrated, got scraped and bruised and shot at, and learned a deep respect for the desert itself. The Sinai is the world's holiest desert, and the most battle-scarred. As the dunes of northern Sinai shifted, I could see pieces of barbed wire, tank treads, an odd shoe, and worn white bones glinting in the sun. The scars of tank tracks crisscrossed the stony plains to the west, and soldiers lay heat-dazed in the sun at the radar station on top of Mount Katerina, just south of Mount Sinai. It would be hard to forget war in this desert.

As Camp David began, I sat at night with the Bedouin smugglers of the northern Sinai, eating crab-apple-sized olives and listening to legends about the stars. I admired these men for their ability to live off the desert, for their knowledge of it, and for their wry tolerance of whatever administration held sway at the time. And then there was their quiet disdain for borders. Wars are fought over borders, and peace is generally a matter of returning to old borders or of establishing new ones. To disdain borders seemed a superior knowledge.

Suspecting that the Sinai border might soon move yet again, these smugglers had discovered a new use for the vagaries of international politics. Mercedes taxis were being stolen in Tel Aviv, driven down to the northern Sinai, and then buried in the dunes under tarpaulins. Time and politics would do the rest. Instead of moving the cars over the border to Egypt, all these men had to do was wait until the border moved over the cars. . . .

The plan was so breathtakingly simple that I could only admire it. The Bedouin never mentioned it to me, nor I to them. To tell how I learned of it would be letting an even bigger cat out of the bag. Enough to say that I kept my peace, and was disgusted a few months later when an ambitious young Tel Aviv journalist broke the story on the front page of his newspaper. Some of the cars were found. I couldn't help hoping that many more were not.

When I got back to Jerusalem, Camp David was still going on — the David of three men up against the Goliath of hate and suspicion. Carter, Sadat and Begin, hidden away in the woods, seemed like three good ole boys determined to have it out behind the woodpile.

As the days went by, the journalists reporting on the meeting seemed far less optimistic than the Bedouin smugglers. Predictions of the outcome became increasingly gloomy. Dan glowered at each news report, refusing as always to bow to accepted opinion. "Listen to them, all those pundits!" he fumed. "There's a blackout on news of the talks, so they don't know what's happening. But they know they have to say *something* when they stand in front of a television camera, so they repeat what they've been telling each other all day in the bar. The only source for all their predictions of failure is themselves!"

As the blackout continued, the journalists went on bluffing, some more convincingly than others. By the following weekend, nearly every journalist of repute — and all those of no repute — had reported the failure of Camp David. The atmosphere was that of vultures hanging over a dying man in the desert, pecking tentatively at him as they waited for the last gasp.

The end came on September 18, 1978, two days before my birthday. I had stayed over at Dan's and we had risen early, since I was due to go back down to the Sinai that day. He was in the bathroom when I turned on the radio to hear the six o'clock news. I heard the first few words:

"Israel and Egypt will sign a peace treaty in three months' time. The treaty will include . . ."

I barely heard the rest of the broadcast. The tears seemed to mist my hearing as well as my vision. The miracle that had been created and then faded into nothingness had come alive again at Camp David. A peace treaty . . .

That was the only item on the news. Dan came in to find me with tears flowing down my face, clutching the radio to me as the morning hymn poured from it. His eyes opened wide in alarm: "What happened?" And I, incapable of coherence, still crying in happiness, just gestured at the radio and said, "The news, the news . . ."

✡

The three months passed, and no treaty was signed. Arik Sharon began creating fake settlements in the northern Sinai in a last-ditch attempt to foil peace. Bo'az graduated as a commander in the tank corps and no longer came home with pockets full of stones. Six months of political maneuvering and tension dried up tears of joy. When the time came to cry again, there were no tears left.

March 26, 1979: the day the peace treaty was finally signed.

We watched the ceremony on the White House lawn by satellite, but it all seemed very small, reduced to the size of the television set. It seemed symbolic that this signing, which would so deeply affect our lives, was taking place thousands of miles away, as if to emphasize the unreality of it for us. The high emotion that came over the satellite from Washington seemed foreign to us in Jerusalem.

As Begin launched into his familiar monologue about the Holocaust, we squirmed, wishing that for once he could allow the present to happen without the past. We listened carefully to Sadat, and watched blank-faced as Carter spoke. Even the weather in Israel seemed to indicate caution. It had turned raw and blustery, with storms and squalls throughout the country, so that relatively few people turned out for the public celebrations. Even in Tel Aviv, where a hundred thousand did gather in the main square, there was no dancing or spontaneity. Everyone was watching the huge video screens set up on the facade of city hall, making sure that it was really happening yet unable somehow to relate to it.

The Americans seemed happier about it all than we were, as though this peace were theirs, not ours. In an entertainment program broadcast on Israel Television after the ceremony, the most joyful sight was that of Zubin Mehta, American flag held high instead of baton, conducting the Israel Philharmonic in an ebullient rendering of "The Stars and Stripes Forever."

Peace with Egypt, a laughable proposition just two years before, had been signed, yet we seemed capable only of a sober comfirmation that it had taken place. Why were we being so blasé, as though we had signed countless peace treaties in our short history as a state?

We were in other, dark places. We were remembering the

dead, among other things. Seven hours before the treaty was signed, a red rose was placed on the grave of every soldier killed in action. But more than that, we feared the future.

The night before the signing, I had a dream. I was living in a small shanty village on top of a volcanic mountain, sharing a house with Menachem Begin. That afternoon, the volcano began to erupt. Many of the villagers packed and fled. I tried to persuade Begin to do likewise. "No," he said. "This is my village, and this is my house. I will not leave."

I felt it would be unfair to leave without him, and besides, by late afternoon the eruption seemed to be ending. The rumblings had quieted down, and although there were a few sparks in the air, there was no sign of lava overflowing.

So in the dream, I stayed. Then in the middle of the night I heard a horrifying sound, a roaring and crackling that surrounded the house. Looking out of the window, I saw rivers of red-hot spitting lava flowing over the mountaintop. The fierce colors of the lava — orange, scarlet, purple, gold — lit up the night sky, radiating heat and danger as the mass rolled inexorably over houses and gardens. There were few houses left standing, and the remaining villagers had all fled. I banged on the door of Begin's room.

"We have to leave now, quickly," I shouted. "The lava has practically cut us off."

He came to the door in a plaid dressing gown, standing very straight and proud. "I will never leave," he said, "not even for a volcano."

Exasperated, I dashed out of the house, saw a narrow opening through the swirling lava, and ran down the mountain just ahead of that molten river, running for my life. At the bottom of the mountain I reached a tunnel, went through it, and emerged into daylight. People were waiting for me there. And as I walked toward them, the mountain behind me became a huge house . . . and collapsed.

I woke in shock. I thought I had been one of the happiest people in the country about the peace treaty, though I was quite aware of its shortcomings, recognizing that the section on autonomy for the West Bank was so vague as to be meaningless. But I had no idea that I might be as wary about peace — as fearful of it — as the many critics of the treaty.

Tentatively, for I was ashamed of my own dream, I told it to a few friends. Like myself, they were part of the Peace Now movement. The Peace Now stickers were still on the rear windows of their cars, as on mine, a happy reminder of what had been achieved. And to my surprise, they were far more accepting of my dream than I. Tamara had had visions of disasters to come, not in dreams but in waking moments throughout the day: "Just walking down the street, I suddenly thought, *What if peace is signed and then war breaks out the next day?*" Udi nodded gloomily: "Sadat took us by surprise once before, and I can't help thinking that this would be a perfect opportunity for him to do it again."

These visions harked back to 1973, to the Yom Kippur War, to an Israel lulled into a false sense of security. They were visions of disaster born out of peace. But they weren't *our* visions, I protested. They were the visions of the opposing camp — of the right-wing firebrand Geula Cohen, of the brutally blind Arik Sharon, of that section of the Israeli population that opposed even signing the treaty, placing its faith in territory instead of in people. It was almost as though we begrudged the peace. Or as though we couldn't grasp it.

People talked of its advantages in negative terms, as had President Carter at the signing ceremony. "The soil of the two lands is not drenched with flowing blood," he'd said. "The

179

countryside of both lands is free from the litter and carnage of wasteful war. Mothers in Egypt and Israel are not weeping today for their children fallen in senseless battle.'' It had all been in terms of what would *not* happen, as though he too could not imagine just what peace would be.

So we were left with a strange emptiness. Just as the opposite of pain is the absence of pain, so now the opposite of war was no longer peace but the absence of war. And that was less than we had expected. The day after the signing, a two-part cartoon ran in *Ha'aretz*. In the first part, Israel was sinking into a stormy sea; in the second, it was in a paper boat labeled ''Peace treaty with Egypt,'' and the boat was tossing helplessly in that same stormy sea.

''Well, at least it's better than war,'' people now said. ''We have to give it a chance.'' Yet they didn't sound too sure. After the sixteen months of uncertainty between the Sadat visit and the actual signing of the treaty, what Israelis wanted even more than peace was a respite from uncertainty, a return to something they knew and could deal with. And peace was an unknown.

✡

I was lucky. I was to experience peace directly. Less than a year after the treaty was signed, I arrived in Egypt on assignment for an American magazine. As the plane landed, I had the strange sensation of stealing into enemy country. By the time it took off, a month later, I was planning ways — as yet unfound — to spend six months in Cairo.

In that month, I had become an honored guest and even a curiosity — a dovish Israeli willing and eager not just to interview but to talk. For the first and only time in my life, I felt like a Jewish princess.

There had been long evenings in a duplex penthouse above the Nile, where cobwebs hid in the corners of the elegantly gilded ceilings and the Persian carpets were worn threadbare, signs of a former grandeur frayed into homeliness. There were stories of the Six Days War — what I had been doing when it broke out, what my Egyptian hosts and their friends had been doing — and I realized with surprise that they too remembered those days with an astonished clarity. The surprise came from what were still the dark recesses of enmity. Enemies, after all, are not real people; they don't think, feel and react the way we do; they are "other." Now these people who had once been enemies, and therefore without feelings, were becoming friends.

We went on swapping stories. I'd had no idea that Cairo was under blackout during the War of Attrition across the Suez Canal in the late sixties, when Israeli planes bombed in-depth, close to the city limits. They'd had little idea of the vast range of legitimate political opinion inside Israel or of the sturdiness of its democracy. Indeed, how could they, in a country where the opposition had a nasty habit of ending up in jail? Together, we wondered openly, even optimistically, how long it would be before Begin was out of power. When it came to Sadat, we talked in hushed voices about his domestic policies and his repression of dissent. But most of the conversation was very familiar. People worried about politics, discussed prices, wrote poetry, complained about tourists, tried to get their children into good schools, told bad jokes, just as in Israel. "Can we trust them?" they asked about Israelis, just as Israelis were asking about them. And the answer they gave each other was inevitably the same as the Israeli one: "We have to give it a chance."

And also as in Israel, not everyone was willing to give peace that chance.

In a deserted restaurant by the Nile, over huge grilled Red Sea shrimp, a Communist who had been jailed several times under both Nasser and Sadat made it clear that he was doing me a favor by talking to me at all. He opposed the peace treaty; it would make Egypt an American puppet, as Israel already was. Whispering, though there was nobody within ten yards of our table, he confided that the real problem was that Sadat imagined he was another pharaoh. But his Communism could not cover his snobbery: "Who does he think he is? He's just the son of a truck driver!" He seemed to resent the fact that Sadat had made history.

That history came to an end the following year, when Sadat was killed by Islamic fundamentalists. I had half expected it to happen, yet I sat in shock when I heard. And though I never thought that I could ever mourn the death of a dictator, I did mourn Sadat's death. I read Bill Farrell's account of it again and again in the *New York Times*. The next time I saw Bill, he'd tell me of his own shock when it happened, before his eyes, as he was covering the parade Sadat was meant to review. "I'd never seen anyone killed before," he said. That was before he was sent to Lebanon. What had struck him above all was the confusion — what had happened, who was hurt, how many, by whom? Death is confusing.

Sadat killed, Begin a hermit in deep depression, Carter returned to Georgia — all three of the signers of that treaty are no longer part of the political scene. Yet to the astonishment of many, the treaty has survived. However great the difficulties surrounding it, and however deep the remaining conflicts, they cannot compete with the supreme self-interest on both sides of those three words: "No more war."

Once the impossible had happened, we learned very quickly to take it for granted. We forgot that we had ever thought it impossible. But it is the memory of that seeming impossibility that makes me refuse the invitation to despair over the situation on the West Bank, even though there are times when despair seems the only logical reaction.

XVI

IT was dry. There had been no rain since the first one, and there was talk of drought. For several days now, the weather service had been forecasting heavy rain, with high winds and hail and thunderstorms. Everyone talked about the disastrous weather on the way, veering from drought to flood with the same excitement of the extreme. But the weather remained obstinately unthreatening. Each morning, I went up onto the roof and scanned the horizon for the mass of black clouds advancing on the city; each morning, all I saw was blue sky. The fine weather became almost oppressive in its refusal to cooperate.

Reading *Ha'aretz* under this persistent sun, I came across a passage written by Chaim Weizmann, the first president of Israel, a few months before the state was founded:

"It is not possible that there should be one constitution for Jews and another for Arabs. We must hold to a principle that was expressed in the Bible: 'There shall be one rule and one law for yourselves and for the stranger that dwells among you.' I am certain that the world will judge the Jewish state by the way it treats the Arabs. . . . Our security will, to a large degree, be dependent not on armies, which we can build, but on the internal stability of our society, which will in turn affect the stability of the state from external forces."

No cloud passed in front of the sun, though I half expected one to do so as I read those lines. This founding father must have been turning in his grave.

Today, in the West Bank, there are two laws in operation — one for Jews and one for Arabs. Jewish settlers live under civilian Israeli law; Palestinians live under military occupation law, which severely curtails their civil rights. Rightwing annexationist Israelis would not have it any other way. Their hope is that life can be made so unpleasant for West Bank Palestinians that they will leave of their own accord. One Jewish Agency spokesman boasts of the high rate of Palestinian emigration from the West Bank, especially among intellectuals who could become political leaders. In response to this, a new policy has developed among West Bank professionals and intellectuals, who have the economic choice of leaving to find more freedom in a country other than their own. The new policy is to remain *samid,* "steadfast." They are determined to stay, using the only kind of vote available to them — their feet — in the hope that someday, a solution can be found.

Two Palestinians were speaking one evening at Tsavta, the tiny West Jerusalem theater club on King George Street, just opposite the Jean Arp sculpture *Three Graces* at the top of Independence Park. Ziyad Abu-Zayyad, a lawyer, is a slim man in his forties with a soft but very definite voice. He used to be the editor of *El Fajr,* the East Jerusalem newspaper that often appears with up to half a page blank due to Israeli military censorship, even of translations of articles that have already appeared in the Hebrew press. Hana Siniora, a decade Abu-Zayyad's senior, is the owner and current editor of *El Fajr,* and in 1985 would become one of the few Palestinians acceptable to both Israel and the PLO in possible negotiations with the United States. The audience was entirely Jewish.

Both men argued for coming to terms. Nothing was irreversible, they said; nothing was ever too late. Roads and houses built in the West Bank by Israelis could be used as easily by Arabs as by Jews. There might even be compensation for the physical settlements. Yet as they went on, a certain desperation began to show through.

Speaking in Hebrew, Abu-Zayyad argued for a binational state. "I hope Israel *will* annex the territories," he said. If that happened, then West Bank Palestinians would become Israeli citizens, would get the vote and use it, and would get enough representatives in the Knesset to form a governing coalition with progressive Israeli parties. "At least that way we'd gain some control over our lives," he explained.

Beside me sat Naomi Kies, a peace activist who had come to Israel the same year I did. I turned to her in confusion. "I don't understand," I whispered. "What's he doing? Is this an argument of desperation, or is he deliberately warning Israelis off annexation, reminding them of the consequences, or is he just making the best of a bad situation?"

She shrugged, as puzzled as I. "I've never heard him argue this before," she said, and then listened in amazement as Abu-Zayyad upped the ante by declaring that if he were Israeli, he'd have voted for the right-wing Likud party, preferring a clear-cut annexationist policy to the same policy masquerading as something else. I smiled. I had heard this argument before — not from Abu-Zayyad, but from Moshe Dayan. In the early seventies, Dayan had gone to Gaza to meet the head of the Red Crescent there, a fervent anti-occupation activist and a man branded as one of Israel's most obstinate enemies in the occupied territories. Just by meeting him, Dayan was breaking government policy. He returned to Tel Aviv saying that if he had to have enemies, he preferred proud dangerous men like that. There, he said, was an enemy he could respect (and an enemy he later deported).

Both Dayan in his time and Abu-Zayyad now have been among the few mainstream public figures to insist on maintaining contact with "the other side." It seems a paradox that such men should prefer their enemies clear-cut. They search for understanding, but mistrust friendship. Perhaps, given the circumstances, they are right.

But this was no time for figuring out paradoxes. A handful of right-wing hecklers in the audience had been incensed by Abu-Zayyad's comments, and three of them were standing with faces reddening and fists waving, matching insult for insult with the rest of the audience. Two of them were Americans, as their accents made clear. The third was from Iraq. He was in his thirties, dark and possibly good-looking were it not for his face being utterly distorted in a caricature of hate. Lips curled and eyes bulging, his whole body stiff with tension, he stared as though looks could really kill.

"What about the Jews who were thrown out of Arab countries? What about them? Answer me. Answer me!" he shouted, repeating the question louder every time Abu-Zayyad or Siniora tried to answer. "I don't want to live next door to a Palestinian state," he declared. "I don't want to! Do *you* want to live side by side with a Jewish state? Hey? Are you ready for that in your Palestinian state?"

"Sure," said Abu-Zayyad. "Of course I am."

The Iraqi glared in fury. The answer had come so quickly and briefly that he hadn't had time to shout it down. "Hand on your heart and tell me you're ready."

"I just told you. Of course I am."

The Iraqi's fury only increased at again getting the answer he didn't want. He was two rows behind me, but I could feel the tension radiating from him. I turned to look and was caught for a moment in that glare of hate. It was terrifying.

He went on shouting. The two Americans joined him in their broken Hebrew. Soon the whole room seemed to be shouting back at them. I would have thought Naomi would be used to such scenes, but she too lost control and joined in. And then just as I felt my own temper rising to the breaking point, I realized that Abu-Zayyad and Siniora were sitting quite still, in the eye of this storm. They were looking on with a gentle, almost humorous patience. I recognized it, and then with relief slipped into it myself. For me, it was a defense against painful involvement, a means of avoiding useless confrontation. But for them it was something else: they knew that this shouting match was not their problem, but ours.

The shouting died down as everyone slowly saw that the speakers were almost the only ones not speaking. The moderator opened the floor to questions, and the well-intentioned dovish majority in the room got their chance. "But what's the solution?" they asked Siniora and Abu-Zayyad. "What's *your* solution? What borders do you see? What kind of Palestinian state? How would it run? Who would run it?" They seemed unaware that if anyone on earth had the answer to all those questions, that person would deserve the Nobel Peace Prize every year of their life until they died. The questions betrayed a soft helplessness; while the right had violent answers, the left was haunted by doubts, questions and seeming impossibilities — by the lack of clear solutions.

The moderator began to sum up. As he talked, the three right-wingers rose, all at the same time, and made for the one exit. I tensed. This was odd. Why were they leaving now? Why not wait a few minutes until the end?

The Iraqi was the last to leave. He planted himself in the doorway and pointed dramatically at the speakers. His finger trembled with anger, and the cords of his neck bulged obscenely as he made his final declaration of the evening: "You'll be sorry you ever came here tonight, I promise you that." He swiveled to include us all in the range of that vengeful finger: "All of you, you'll all be sorry. But you —" with a hiss, the finger stabbing toward Abu-Zayyad — "you especially. This I promise you."

The tension in me broke into relief as I realized that if he'd had a gun, he'd have used it by now. I knew that hate, and I knew where it could lead. It was the same hate that had begun to distort this country, the hate fostered by Begin and Sharon and Kahane, the hate that had killed Emil Grunzweig.

That too had begun peacefully enough: a Peace Now march through the streets of Jerusalem. The official report on the Sabra and Shatila massacres had just held the Begin government negligent and indirectly responsible. On that cold night of February 1983, Peace Now was demanding that the government resign.

The marchers were like most of the audience that evening of Tsavta; they were "the beautiful Israel," the cream of the society: reserve army officers, students, professionals and intellectuals. They were left of center, upper middle-class, and almost entirely Ashkenazic — of eastern European origin.

They were met by fervent supporters of the Begin government bused in from the nearby development town of Beit Shemesh, a backwater peopled predominantly by Sephardic Israelis of Middle Eastern and North African origin. For the length of the route, the counterdemonstrators harassed the marchers. "You professors, you . . . you lecturers!" they screamed, hurling the tags like curses while others chanted, "Begin, King of Israel!"

"They should have burned you all in the ovens at Auschwitz!" screamed one. "PLO lovers! You should have been with your friends in Sabra and Shatila so they could have killed you too!'' yelled another.

Verbal violence escalated into physical violence. The Peace Now marchers were spat at, punched and kicked. One counterdemonstrator grabbed the collar of a political-science student in the front line of the march and thrust his face into the student's. Spittle flew from his mouth as he delivered his message: ''You wait. We'll kill you before this night is out!''

An hour later, outside the prime minister's office, a hand grenade was thrown into the crowd of Peace Now demonstrators. Emil Grunzweig, that political-science student, was killed on the spot.

✡

Passion pulls the pin on the grenade, but it can also trigger the search for peace. Meron Benvenisti, for instance, is a passionate man. His passion is coexistence.

Benvenisti's work accounted for the relative ease with which East and West Jerusalem were reunited after 1967, when Mayor Teddy Kollek appointed him the municipal administrator of the Old City and East Jerusalem. In those heady years when all still seemed possible, he worked for more than physical reunification. The results of that work can still be seen.

Upper-class young people from Arab East Jerusalem venture into the nightlife of the Jewish West, trying out the Cinemateque and the Tsrif. West Jerusalemites flock to East Jerusalem restaurants, especially at Passover, when they can get bread there. Both Arabs and Jews vote in municipal elections. Young Arab families go to the municipal swimming pool in the German Colony, and picnic in the parks. Arabs and Jews work side by side at the watermelon stands outside Damascus Gate, on assembly-line jobs, and in Hadassah Hospital, where patients as well as nurses are both Arab and Jewish. But there is a basic distortion: the East serves the West. Hotel waiters and chambermaids, sewage, sanitation and construction workers, house painters and municipal gardeners and porters, are almost all Arab. East Jerusalem is now ringed by new Jewish suburbs, and Arab Jerusalemites feel hemmed in. Social relationships are limited mainly to homosexual pickups and to prostitution, which has its own strange rules: though Jewish prostitutes will accept Arab clients, Arab prostitutes refuse Jews.

The city seems united on the surface, but the social, administrative and political divisions run deep. Jerusalem is still a peaceful place compared with other divided cities such as Belfast or Beirut, to be sure, but those two cities haunt Benvenisti's visions. "There is no place which arouses such deep fanatical feelings as Jerusalem," he wrote in 1976. "The city's atmosphere nurtures an exclusive possessiveness. . . . This is the only place in the world today where Arabs and Jews live side by side, and where the struggle is a real, everyday occurrence and not an abstraction. He who decides to judge between the two sides must remember that only in fairy tales is one side all good and the other all bad."

But few people can remember that. Benvenisti resigned his post as deputy mayor in frustration shortly after he wrote those words, after the rejection of his proposal for a borough system of city administration similar to London's. No longer in any executive position, he began research and founded the West Bank Database Project, which keeps tabs on what is happening with Jewish settlement in the West Bank.

For some years, his data have shown that Jewish settlement and land appropriation were nearing the stage of de facto annexation of the West Bank. By 1984, more than half the land there was under direct Israeli ownership, one way or another. (The following year, the state comptroller would find that the majority of private Jewish acquisition of land in the West Bank was achieved through a mixture of fraud and intimidation.) Things were rapidly approaching the point of no return for Israel in the territories, said Benvenisti. And with that he gained a reputation as the man who declared that the settlement process was "irreversible."

Israeli settlement officials praised his work to the heavens. "Ignore his politics," one told me, "because his data are absolutely correct. We couldn't have done a better job ourselves." The right was delighted at his findings, using them to back its claim that the West Bank could no longer be returned to anyone, and that it was now and would remain "Jewish."

Such praise from unexpected quarters put Benvenisti in the tragic situation of having his work used to serve the interests of those he opposed. He became a target of many doves, who accused him of spreading defeatism and despair and of playing into the hands of the right.

As often happens, the facts of the matter were somewhat different. Benvenisti never used the word *irreversible* about Jewish settlement on the West Bank. I know that for sure, because the word first came into the public domain in a conversation between myself and that same settlement official who was so delighted with Benvenisti's work: one Ze'ev Ben-Yosef, deputy head of the settlement division of the World Zionist Organization, the main planning body for Israeli settlement in the West Bank. It was in October 1983.

We had been poring over maps in his office — "secret" maps of his department's thirty-year plan, which blithely called for the same number of Jews as Arabs to be living in the West Bank by the year 2010 (a plan since made moot by Israel's disastrous economic situation, because whatever the politics involved, Israel simply cannot afford continued settlement in the West Bank). The maps were all over the place: spread out on the table, hung behind a large green curtain on the wall, tucked away in typewritten reports for a few privileged eyes only. As I looked at them, I traced the Green Line in my mind. It had to be in my mind, because it wasn't on the maps.

Ben-Yosef was rhapsodizing about the prospect of a Jewish Judea and Samaria — the biblical names for the West Bank and, since Begin took office in 1977, the official ones too. "Physically, any withdrawal from Judea and Samaria is now impossible," he said with relish. "The situation there is now irreversible."

The word sounded oddly clinical in Hebrew. I asked what he meant by it.

"Irreversible," he ventured, "is like when you've had a really bad head injury — let's say you've fallen off a horse or something — and the blood stops flowing to the brain. Well, if the brain gets no blood for over a certain amount of time, the damage caused is irreversible."

It was a surprisingly sharp image. Was Israel suffering irreversible brain damage? Was that the way he saw it?

"Oh, no," he said quickly, suddenly aware of the implication of his own analogy. "Of course here it's quite the reverse. Here we're making a sick body into a healthy one."

Yet the analogy haunted me as I drove around the West Bank afterward, seeing what had changed since the last time I'd written about the settlements, in early 1978. Now as then, it was an unpleasant trip for me. The settlers were mainly religious Jews who used their religiousness to justify racism. And though it should come as no surprise that there are Jews as capable of racism as anyone else, it was hard for me to sit and listen to their rationalizations — and even harder when it was later revealed that the Jewish terrorists got their rabbis'

193

approval before acting, just as in Iran the revolutionaries got the approval of their ayatollahs.

The West Bank doesn't seem like land that would arouse too much passion. Samaria, the northern part of it, is a place of stone hills with so little earth that even after thousands of years of terracing there is soil enough only for olive trees. At times it can feel like Greece, until you round another bend in the road and see yet another new settlement sitting squat and fortresslike on top of a hill, behind its ring of barbed wire.

The largest of these fortresses, and one of the few without barbed wire, so confident is it in its size and indestructibility, is Ariel, the capital of Jewish Samaria. In early 1978, Ariel consisted of three temporary huts staked out on the hilltop. It was called Haris then, after the Arab village on the slope of the hill opposite. There had been nobody in the huts, and the whole idea of a capital city here had seemed laughable. Now Ariel is a sprawling township, with apartment houses and villas spilling down the sides of the hilltop and about to spread over the next two hills. The villas are a jumble of homeowners' dreams. Ultramodern sits within spitting distance of Swiss chalet, ranch house within a whisper of Disneyland castle. A sociologist of middle-class fantasies could have a field day with this architecture.

At least Yaacov Feitelson, the head of the town council, knows the names of the Arab villages we could see from his hilltop office. Most of the settlers don't; they act as though the villages don't exist. Feitelson pointed to the most striking feature of the landscape to the north of Ariel: a lone apartment house on top of the highest hill in Samaria, some ten miles away. "That's Moshe Zar's," he said admiringly. "Just bought the land from Arabs and built his own private fortress up there. That was my dream once too — my own private fortress on top of a hill. Well, so now I have Ariel instead."

Feitelson came to Israel from Russia in 1972, after a few months in jail for his association with a group that attempted to hijack an airliner out of Leningrad. He had opposed the attempt but was jailed anyway. In Israel, he wanted to "build the country" in the old Zionist sense, to start something new. But it had to be something big: "I don't believe in small things. They don't work." After standing for the Knesset in 1977 as a member of Arik Sharon's Shlomzion party (he didn't get in, and Sharon quickly dived back into the Likud), Feitelson joined the settlement group that would establish Ariel.

He was proud of all this, and happy to talk about it. But after an hour or so, as he began boasting about his sense of realpolitik, the talk took an unexpected turn. "Listen," he said, "I sympathize with the Arabs here. I came from a conquered country, from Latvia, so I know what it's like. Now there's two ways the conqueror can deal with things. One is to shoot and kill and imprison, like the British did in their empire. And the other is to do as the Russians did: give them their own culture, their own language, a decent standard of living and local autonomy, and keep full control over all the really important things."

Such admiration for the Russian way of doing things seemed odd from a man who had been imprisoned in Russia. How did it feel now that he was in the place of the Russians?

He hunched down over his desk and rubbed his hands together in only slightly embarrassed delight. "Wonderful!" he said.

✡

Those who do not think it so wonderful are haunted by a sense of failure. Meron Benvenisti's curly hair is completely gray by now, and he has gained bulk over the years. But he still has the energy of a thin man, and the fire of one who obstinately refuses to give in.

We sat in the study of his home in Abu Tor, in the first house over the 1967 border. Built high into the rock of the mountainside, the house commands the stunning classic view of the gold- and silver-domed mosques and the Mount of Olives beyond — an East Jerusalem view. The maps lining Benvenisti's office are even more detailed than those in Ben-Yosef's.

I listened, making notes, as he outlined the latest annual report of the Database Project, which was still at the printer's. "It will look something like this," he said, handing me a blue paperback that turned out to be the latest report of the South African Institute on Race Relations.

He spoke with an intensity very similar to that of the West Bank settlers, except that where theirs was ebullient and hopeful, his was close to despair. He nodded when I pointed that out. "My whole generation — people going into their fifties — is going through it. Our parents brought us up to be normal people and to make miracles. I know that's a contradiction, but that's how we were brought up here. And instead of making miracles, look at what we've done. We've had no influence on how the country has developed. Oh, we're good people and fine people to be sure, but basically we're out of touch with what's really happening in the country. You know all those liberal Israelis who go around saying that they carry a passport to a country that no longer exists? What do they mean, it no longer exists? Of course it exists. But *they* no longer exist *in* it. It's they who are missing, not the country."

It's not enough, he said, to sit around on Friday nights crying on each other's shoulders and eating cake. Tears would change nothing. Neither would a determination to ignore the facts of de facto annexation of the West Bank, or the attacks on himself as the messenger who should be blamed for bringing the bad news. "The fact is that we liberals are out of contact with our own country, and we have to reestablish that contact, to take an active part again, to regain influence."

The difficult part is that most Israelis really couldn't care less about what is happening on the West Bank. "They don't go there and they don't think about it. Now some analysts see this as a sign that they reject it, but that's not so. Quite the contrary. They accept it as part of the normal state of affairs, and go there as much and as little as they go to the Galilee or to the Negev. It's an accepted part of the country and that's it. It's become normal." De facto psychological annexation.

The more he talked, the more Meron reminded me of Jacobo Timerman, the Argentinian journalist who had been imprisoned and tortured in his own country, released to Israel, and had then left Israel in disappointment. There was that same feeling of a prophet shouting in the wilderness, that same untidy bulk and impassioned energy. But with Meron there seemed to be a deeper, more lingering pain. He gave a rueful shrug when I made the comparison, and quickly established the difference between himself and Timerman. "I was born in Jerusalem," he said, "and I'll die here."

Meanwhile he continues the long sorry act of record keeping. He has become the bookkeeper of colonization, of land expropriations, purchases and zonings. He records the technical details of history as it happens. The historians will thank him, but for him it is clear that this is a completely thankless task.

A sense of failure crept over me as I sat across the desk from him. As the Israeli administration encroached on Arab

lands, so the whole seemingly inexorable process of change —
from a secular, humanist, socialist society to a religious right-
wing one — began to encroach on my mind.

It was as though I were in a gigantic game of Othello, where
two opponents, one with white marbles and the other with
black, invade each other's territory until one is finally pushed
right off the board. I had never been very good at the game.
Whenever I played, choosing the white marbles if I could,
the black marbles would slowly and relentlessly surround mine,
crowding me into a corner without my even quite realizing
how it had happened. I always knew that if I sat back and
quietly analyzed the game, I might do better. But I was too
busy protecting an individual marble here and there, going off
in minor false directions, to be able to protect my major interests. I sat there wondering if Meron would be any better at
the game than I, or if we were both ineffective players.

"It wouldn't hurt so much if it wasn't for the nostalgia,"
he said as I got up to leave. I knew what he meant. It wasn't
even so much the nostalgia for what was, as the nostalgia for
what might have been — for the years when everything still
seemed possible, and when we didn't have to grasp at memory to remind ourselves that nothing was ever impossible.

The prophets of doom tend to be buried by the apparently
indomitable human ability to simply muddle on through. I knew
this, yet in the face of the facts, the thought was cold comfort. Could I really conceive of coming back here? Of coming back to watch the place I loved being taken over by those
I was beginning to hate? But then leaving was just as hard.
How could I find the stoicism to watch from a distance, and
how live with myself for having given up on a whole country?

I stood on the steps outside Meron's house, looking at the
gold and silver domes. This holiness had once entranced me;

now it was beginning to repel me. The bond between holiness and fanaticism was too strong. The sacred brought about the profane in this country; it always has, and it still does.

Those years between 1948 and 1967 had been tough, sparse years for those who lived here then, but they had also been years of a new dream, years when it seemed that a modern, secular Jerusalem could escape the fate of its history. Perhaps, after all, that dream really had been impossible. Perhaps that Irish shepherd was right: Jerusalem was no place for the likes of me. It was a city of prayer and blood, faith and violence — a cruel, holy city. Perhaps it was simply too late to come back. The country had gone too far in one direction, and I in another. But I knew I couldn't decide yet.

Water wears down even stone, I remembered, and the stream of history wears down individual hopes, memories and loves. A familiar overwhelming weariness came over me.

XVII

DAYS began to blend into each other as the time for me to leave came closer. The leaves of the Persian lilac outside my door had long fallen; only the hard whitish berries remained, glowing golden in the late afternoon sun. Bees flew into my room, flying low and settling on the windowsills to die. It was autumn, cold at night and by day hot in the sun and chilly in the shade. It was the season of confusion.

Worlds collided. I picked up a magazine in Jerusalem and found an article I had written the previous summer in Maine. I told Ilana about carved American eagles hanging from the beams of an old lighthouse, about the mist closing in as I scrambled over the rocks and the bell buoy sounding forlornly through the white night of fog. But the memories sounded strange under the pine trees of her garden. Dislocated. My knee began to hurt again.

Letters arrived from friends in New York, full of professional gossip and bubbling with that particularly hyper New York vitality. The paperback cover of my last book arrived, gaudy and iridescent, with apologies from my publishers anticipating my reaction. (The apologies were unnecessary: I loved it.) News came that I would be teaching the following spring at a university in the American Northwest — a country of water and forests, as different from this one as any country could be.

Somewhere else, in utterly different places, a professional me had a full and busy life. Yet I felt so comfortable here. It was as though there were two of me, one professional and one personal, and we had carelessly let it come to pass that we lived thousands of miles away from each other, in different cities, different countries and different continents. For a moment I thought of the vast geological movements of continents, huge plates of land swinging away from each other over billions of years. I imagined my life as a reverse flow of plate tectonics, bringing continents together. But then I looked at Ilana's face and saw the sense of distance suddenly written there. Her awareness of my existence in another place had entered between us, pushing us apart, saying, "Whoa! Hold on there! You think you're at home here? Then what's all this? You exist elsewhere."

The world seemed both very large and very small, and so did I.

My lawyer called from New York; my visa to reenter the United States had come through. I felt an immense relief — I had the choice again. Yet at the same time there was a sense of disappointment; the choice itself can be burdensome.

An easy comfort had developed with Ya'ir over the past few weeks. It was not the kind of impassioned involvement I had known in the past, but something far more relaxed and far less demanding. I kept warning myself against romance. This too had not been planned for. "What will happen if you fall in love with someone in Jerusalem?" a friend had asked before I left New York. I had laughed: "No danger of that. That only happens when you want it to, and I don't want it to, not now, not there." Or did I?

The assurance of what I had said then was disappearing. I no longer knew just what I wanted. "I can't fall in love, I'm meant to be leaving," I protested to myself. Yet something was clearly developing between Ya'ir and myself — something gentle and strong at the same time, and something with far more patience than the passionate immediacy of falling in love.

Ya'ir wondered if he would have allowed this to happen if he hadn't known that I was leaving again. I wondered the same thing about myself. My departure date had been our safeguard against involvement, the defense mechanism of two wary, private people who had only allowed themselves to come together when they knew it was temporary. Yet now it seemed that we had both overestimated my determination to leave.

We began to strain against each other, searching out differences to focus on. I liked the sun, he the shade; I liked the Tsrif at Friday lunchtime, he liked the Ben-Yehuda Street cafés. He had been born in Jerusalem — had been raised here, had fought here, and had lived here all his life. I had lived on three continents and seemed to be in perpetual motion. We were opposites, and though it is true that opposites attract, they also clash.

The clash was clearest when it came to politics. After all, this was Israel. And though we voted the same way, we reacted differently to what was happening. That became clear one night when the television news broadcast a Syrian-made videotape of an eighteen-year-old girl who had carried out a suicide bombing against Israeli troops in Lebanon, killing thirteen soldiers together with herself. The tape had been made a few hours before she executed her mission.

It was horribly fascinating. This young woman had been beautiful, well-spoken, lucid, and a fervent nationalist. She was not a religious fanatic, as the Israelis had hitherto assumed all suicide bombers to be. Nor was she ignorant or afraid, as were many of the would-be bombers who had panicked at the last moment and given themselves up to Israeli troops. Her mission, she said, was "to get the enemy out of

southern Lebanon, to free my land from enemy occupation."
A Pasionaria of action.

I watched the tape together with Ya'ir and his neighbors, a couple our age; she had been born and raised on a kibbutz, and he, like Ya'ir, in Jerusalem. But they all seemed indifferent to that fatal combination of beauty, patriotism and suicidal fantasy. As we watched, reading the Hebrew subtitles to her calm cadence in Arabic, I remarked that if I were eighteen and living in southern Lebanon, I'd be wishing that I too could be a suicide bomber.

"Come on," said Ya'ir, "you've got to be joking. Those people are crazy."

"I know, but it's the kind of craziness that's attractive when you're young and idealistic," I argued. "It's heady stuff. It's a grand gesture, taking others with you when you go, and it has a huge drama to it. Look at her — she knows that we'll be seeing this when she's already dead, and she's actually enjoying that. She knows she's going to do what she set out to do."

"But you'd never really do something like that."

"No, I wouldn't, but I can understand it. To be eighteen and have this fervent sense of idealism, plus this feeling that you've got nothing to lose . . ."

"What idealism? They know we're leaving Lebanon in any case."

"How do they know? They know we're talking about it, that's all. And they know Arik Sharon's talking against leaving because it will only be difficult to get back in again. He actually *likes* being there. They want to make sure we really do leave."

The girl on the screen was still talking. Now she was asking forgiveness of her mother and father, begging them to be proud of her and to understand her. If I had been Lebanese,

I might have been in tears by now. "Some very clever person made this tape," I said. "Somebody expert at manipulation and propaganda. Kids will be lining up to be suicide bombers now."

"It's a good thing they're not all like you," joked the neighbor. "There's enough craziness in this part of the world." Ya'ir just looked at me suspiciously, as though at any moment I might get into a car packed with explosives and drive right into him. (Sure enough, the following months would produce a slew of young suicide bombers operating against Israeli forces in Lebanon, all of whom first immortalized themselves on camera.)

As the inevitable analyst came on screen to discuss the tape, I wondered at this flat dismissal of crazy idealism. Of course it was foreign to this generation of Israelis. When I was eighteen and marching for nuclear disarmament in England, they were just going into the Israeli army. They never had those heady years that are the luxury of youth in a peaceful society — the years of the sixties in England and the States, with the freedom to explore different ways of seeing the world. While I wore my hair long and dressed in army-and-navy surplus, their hair was cropped short and they wore battle fatigues. While I had all the freedom I wanted, they were in the strict routine of army training. While I hiked and hitched my way around Europe, they were doing forced marches in the Negev desert. I was discovering idealism in a country that had been sovereign for a thousand years, while they were living in a small beleaguered country that was younger than they were.

Yet that country was itself founded by crazy idealistic teenagers. Most of the socialist Zionists who came here in the early part of this century were seventeen-, eighteen- and nineteen-year-olds, rebels against their middle-class backgrounds in eastern Europe. They were attracted to the physical hardships of Palestine at that time, and imbued with the drama and excitement of building a new country. But now the country is already built. And the idealism has changed. This being the Middle East, it takes strange forms.

In Lebanon, a country seemingly bent on self-destruction, the young idealist could find no better outlet than her own self-destruction. That is the idealism of desperation. In Israel, there is the government-sponsored idealism of West Bank settlement, but that is attractive only to the right-wing and the religious. There seems to be a dearth of constructive idealism. And even those who want it don't seem to know how to find it.

✡

In the main music store on Ben-Yehuda Street, a young man sat on a stool near the door, gently strumming a guitar and humming to himself. As my shadow fell over the guitar, he looked up at me dreamily, smiled, and went on playing. There was nobody else in the store.

The gentleness was infectious, and the noise of the pedestrian mall outside seemed suddenly far away. I listened awhile to his music. "Do you work here?" I asked finally.

He looked up again. "Yes," he said, and seemed to laugh. Then he gently put the guitar aside and asked me what it was I wanted. I was an easy customer. A gift certificate for a bar mitzvah present, I said. I wrote out the check, he wrote out the certificate, and I put both check and certificate into my purse. This time he laughed out loud. "Perhaps you should leave the check with me," he said. I blushed with embarrassment and confusion. He just kept smiling and said not to worry. As I left he sat down again to his guitar. Soft eyes looked up at me once more. "Come back," he said. "Come listen to some music."

I went drifting out into the street, gentled by all that gentleness, the more seductive here because so unusual. You get used to elbowing and shouting for attention in a store, to impatient salespeople and quick brusque transactions with constant interruptions from people behind you trying to buy something at the same time. This man seemed to be from another Israel — a third Israel, as it were, a whole stratum of young people who were neither religious nor ultranationalist. Patient, quiet and gentle, they followed a different way of being that seemed to have grown in the years since I had left. Many of my friends' children were among them.

At Orna and Amir's that same afternoon, I lay back in an old dentist's chair, half in the shade of a pomegranate tree, with my feet in the sun and a glass of sage tea in my hand. One of Orna's cats leaped onto my stomach, then sprang off after a bird just flown from the lemon tree, the other side of the tiny courtyard.

Orna and Amir had been young children when I first knew them. Now they were adults, and somehow, despite the difference in ages, we were the same generation. Their army service behind them, they were both students, he of medicine and she of philosophy. They had just come back from a ten-day yoga "intensive" at a kibbutz in the Galilee.

Orna has long dark hair and strong features, Amir curly blond hair and blue eyes. They could both be straight out of a Leon Uris novel. But they are not the proud fighter types. The fifties image of the "sabra" so earnestly promoted by Uris and others has long since disappeared as the wars became more complex and the sense of right and wrong less clear. Nobody in Israel uses the word *sabra* anymore. They say "Israeli-born" instead.

We talked about what I began to call "the gentle layer" of

Israeli youth. They are a minority, but a conspicuous one. You see them in the Cinemateque, at the Tsrif, at the big Peace Now demonstrations, at the Acre Theater Festival — young women in flowing cotton skirts and loose blouses, young men in cotton pants and tunics, with books or sketch pads under their arms, loose and calm. They seem a gentle answer to the intrusive aggressiveness that is so often the style of Israeli life. They could have come out of the American sixties, perhaps, but these are no flower children. They have all served in the army, they all do reserve service, and most of the men have had to serve in Lebanon. Once you know this, their gentleness takes on something of protest. It is hard to remain gentle in the midst of harshness, and to keep your voice soft when everyone around you seems to shout. It takes a deliberate effort. At times, the soft-spokenness even seems exaggerated, too good to be true. Or perhaps in the Middle East you learn to mistrust gentleness.

Amir just smiled at this idea. Orna thought about it, sitting cross-legged on the straw mat beside me. "I think it comes from a certain despair," she said, "despair at ever doing anything that will have an influence. You begin to ask, 'What difference does it make what I do? What chance do I have of changing this society?' And you see the way things are going and conclude that there's none. So then you create your own standards, your own life, separate from the mainstream one."

I knew what she meant. I could see the attractiveness of it, yet it worried me. It meant that a whole sector of young Israelis were simply withdrawing from the political reality.

"Not withdrawing, really," she said. "It's more like non-involvement. I mean, if something comes up in your personal life, some instance of racism or something, you'll speak out, but only when it's necessary. You won't seek out political activity."

"There's a heavy price to pay for that," I pointed out. I

meant the political price, but she took it personally: "Sure there's a price. There's a certain guilt over retreating from the political arena and leaving it to the extremists of the right. But you see, I think we see ourselves as a vanishing species, threatened with extinction, so we withdraw in order to protect ourselves."

However much I understood, there still seemed to be a profound cynicism behind this demonstrative gentleness. It was the spirit of *rosh katan*, "keeping a small head," that had grown out of the Lebanon war and now seemed to afflict more and more Israelis. The idea was to keep your head down, not to put yourself in the way of trouble, and tend your own garden, raising high the honeysuckle and jasmine so as not to see beyond the fence. It was a spirit of tiredness — a middle-aged spirit among young people just out of regular army service, young people who had been to too many funerals recently and who saw no point in dying in a war they couldn't believe in.

Popular singer Arik Einstein's record *Pesek Zman*, "Time Out," spoke for them. "I want to take some time out and not think," he sang, "to sit down by the sea and not worry, to let my head rest from the explosions, my heart rest from the pressures. . . . Perhaps it's just a small crisis and will pass with time, or perhaps I've just become so very tired." He is the polar opposite of his namesake, Arik Sharon. And those who listen to the one Arik do not listen to the other.

The truth was that I envied Orna and Amir and others like them. Here were people who were managing to lead their lives almost entirely within the other Jerusalem, the one of soft breezes and golden late-afternoon light. I envied their ability to cut themselves off from the politics and the ugliness, even while I saw how dangerous that was.

I still have no idea what makes people react one way or

another. I know that some come out of the army with this almost iron resolve to be gentle, and that others come out having bought into the ideology of muscle and power. Some of my friends' children have done that too.

The week before, I had been in the Mahane Yehuda market off Jaffa Road. Municipal elections were to take place soon, and Arik Sharon was scheduled to tour the market, drumming up support for one of his henchmen. I stood by a vegetable stall to watch as he began his grand progress through the narrow alleys.

The stall-owner tugged gently at my arm. "Come stand here behind the potatoes," he said. "You'll see better from here."

I looked at him in surprise. "You're not going out to greet Arik?"

He shrugged. "We'll give him a nice enough welcome, but that's all. Everyone thinks the market is solidly for Arik because we're all Sephardic here and the Sephardics are meant to be right-wing." He made a gesture as though spitting into the air. "What do they know?"

He was right. I had expected a riot of welcome for Sharon, with mass cries of "Arik, King of Israel!" and people being trampled in the alleys. But the only people shouting that infamous chant were the henchmen he brought with him. Most of the stall owners stayed right where they were, like my newfound friend. They shook hands, exchanged pleasantries as they would with any politician, and went right on selling spices and vegetables. (None of which prevented the television camera from zooming in close, so that on the news that night it looked as though the whole of Mahane Yehuda was ecstatically pro-Sharon.)

The small procession went on up the alley, the stall owner gave me a couple of apples to see me on my way, and I began to follow on behind. Suddenly a tall, broad figure blocked my vision. "Lesley!" said a familiar voice. "What are you doing here?"

I looked up. "Adi! What are *you* doing here?"

I knew that Adi had signed up with the Shin Bet (General Security Services) after army service in order to earn money for university studies. "He travels all over the world," his parents had proudly told me. But neither they nor I had any idea as to exactly what he was doing. Slowly it dawned on me: "Adi, you're not this man's bodyguard?"

He didn't say anything, just grinned down at me.

"But how can you, Adi? Are you being punished or something?"

"It's all part of the job," he said quickly. "Rotating duty. Where are you staying? Mishkenot? I'll call you." He gave me a quick hug — a fleeting impression of iron instead of flesh, all the muscles steel-hard — and was gone off into the crowd around Sharon, leaving me standing there in shock. Adi, little Adi, guarding Sharon? Ready to take bullets intended for that man? I resolved to say nothing to his parents, who were spending that year in the States. Their only son, the brightest in his class at the best high school in Jerusalem, doing a job like this . . . It would break their hearts.

He did call me a couple of weeks later, and we did see each other, but we didn't do too much talking. He was tight-lipped and guarded. "I'm just doing what needs to be done," he said. "I like this way of life. I don't have any complaints. Education can wait." He seemed another person altogether from the bright, optimistic youth who had sat beside me at the Passover table six years before, celebrating peace with Egypt.

XVIII

O N the first night of Passover, every year, the streets of Israel are practically empty. You don't have to be religious to sit down at the *seder* table here; you only have to be Jewish. So just about every Jewish Israeli, no matter how secular, reads at least part of the Haggadah, the Passover service, taking in once again the biblical story of the Exodus from Egypt.

Each year, the Haggadah commands us to see ourselves "as if we had personally gone out of Egypt" — each and every one of us personally oppressed and then saved. It is a freedom tale of victory over the oppressors. And until 1977, in a country that had been through five wars with Egypt in the space of a generation and a half, it made sense. It was a perfect acting-out of whatever was happening with Egypt at the time, an ancient legend with an ever-ready code to the current conflict (a code so strong that nobody was ever able to convince Menachem Begin that the Jews did not build the pyramids, as the Haggadah says they did).

It is a happy service, held *en famille* around the dining table, with lots of food in the middle and lots of wine throughout. By the time it's over, the table is littered with matzoh crumbs, the children are asleep in their mothers' laps, the wine stains have soaked well into the tablecloth, and everyone is slightly hoarse from singing.

The singing is important. That's what makes it a communal affair. That's what makes it fun. And so the service is full of phrases, verses and poems that have a multitude of tunes, all traditional, some crude and repetitive, others lilting and haunting, some just plain rowdy and joyous.

One verse in particular always stays in my head for days afterward, popping into my mind as I wait for a stoplight or brush my teeth in the morning. It is sung with wineglass lifted, to a pretty little tune that belies the impact of the words:

"Not only one rose up against us to destroy us, but in each and every generation they rise up against us to destroy us, and the Holy One blessed be He saves us from them."

For years, those words seemed to be a horrible prophecy, especially with regard to Egypt. A truth dormant through thousands of years had risen to haunt Israel again in the twentieth century, in the very country that was founded to break that tradition of persecution and to release us from the prophecy. Egypt's enmity seemed a dark black joke on the Jews, as though Jehovah were some vengeful Greek god on Olympus, determined to wreak havoc on mere human plans to thwart fate.

And if Egypt does not rise up against us to destroy us, what then? In 1979, with the peace treaty, we lost an old enemy. Old enemies die slowly, true, and there were plenty of enemies left, but it was the accepted wisdom at the time that with Egypt outside the circle of war, the other Arab states would not be strong enough to attack. For the first time in its short modern history, it looked as though Israel might have the basic security it had been longing for.

Yet in 1982, another war began — one of Israel's own choosing. With the invasion of Lebanon, Israel planned to destroy the Palestinian foe. It didn't go according to plan. By the third weary year of that war, the Palestinians were becoming increasingly unsatisfactory as an enemy; there were many signs of moderation within the PLO. But by then a new enemy had risen up against us: the Shiites of southern Lebanon. Though they originally welcomed the Israeli invasion as a means of helping them in their own battle against the PLO, they had now become Israel's most bitter opponent, staging suicide attacks and ambushes that claimed more Israeli casualties by the day.

The long story of how it happened, despite intelligence warnings and the best efforts of experts in the field, has not been told. Many fear it never will be, since there is considerable pressure inside Israel to avoid a commission of inquiry into the Lebanon war such as the one that took place after the Yom Kippur War. The available facts of the matter are bad enough, in particular the news that simulation games played by the top army brass before the war had predicted its results with terrible precision, down to almost the exact number of casualties. Arik Sharon, then defense minister, had seen the reports on those simulation games but launched the war nevertheless. And as Israel prepared to withdraw from Lebanon three years later, it seemed determined to leave behind as much hard feeling as possible. An ''iron-fist'' policy was started, including dawn raids on villages in which the men were herded into the main square to be questioned, orders were given to shoot at anything that moved, and houses were searched with guns blazing. Thousands of Shiites were arrested without charge, and hundreds would later be taken over the border to Israeli prisons, leading to the hijacking of TWA flight 847 in June 1985 and the seventeen-day tension as American passengers were held hostage.

Long before Israel withdrew from Lebanon, there was almost total consensus among Israelis that the war had been a bad mistake. In fact, Arik Sharon seemed to be the only one defending it. Everyone else wanted out of Lebanon as quickly as possible.

"I don't understand," I said to Oded during one of our lunches at the Tsrif, as we discussed a possible subject for his next column. "If someone were to look at it logically, they'd have to assume that Israeli policy during the withdrawal is designed to make enemies of the Shiites, and not just ordinary run-of-the-mill enemies, but the solid kind that last for generations."

"I almost wish you were right," he replied gloomily. "At least that would imply some intelligence behind it all. It would mean there *was* a policy, however bad, and that steps were taken to achieve it. But you're wrong. It's just stupidity. Just an incredible amount of plain stupidity."

"But that kind of stupidity doesn't arise in a vacuum, Oded. It comes from something else — a history of too many enemies, perhaps. We're used to having enemies. Perhaps we even need them."

They were thoughts of a dark day, thoughts of either cynicism or despair, I'm not sure which, though sometimes I suspect the two may be the same. Somehow the Lebanon war seemed perfectly appropriate for the time. Everything seemed to be coming apart.

The death toll on the roads was still rising. Twice as many Israelis were killed on the roads during the Lebanon war as in the war itself. If a man was driving particularly recklessly, people would say that he'd just come back from reserve service in Lebanon. They were only half joking. Inflation was reaching for 1,000 percent, black-market dollars were being hoarded in every home, and burglaries rose alarmingly as a consequence. A newly published book of cartoons listed a thousand and one places to hide cash dollars. Once it had been under a loose floor tile or in the freezer, but now far greater ingenuity was required. The book was a best-seller. Nobody laughed at jokes about Lebanon, least of all the one about how to tell a terrorist (the answer: Shoot — if you kill him, he's a terrorist, if you miss, he's not). "Things fall apart, the center cannot hold" — the same line of Yeats was quoted to me three times in one day. As funeral followed funeral on the television news, the weather remained obstinately sunny. On top of everything else, it was drought.

We had become a country too used to living by force of arms, and too used to the presence of death. The unshakable ghost of the Holocaust, the increasing numbers of war dead, the self-induced massacres on the roads — all could make you think there was a cult of death here, an ironic modern equivalent to the ancient Egyptian one. We are very good at death. We even celebrate death days, not birthdays. The Americans have Lincoln's Birthday and Washington's Birthday; the Israelis have Ben-Gurion Day, but that is the day he died. We are better at solemnity than at rejoicing, or perhaps we just have more experience of it. It's a habit, a way of thinking. The *kaddish* for the dead is the best-known prayer in Judaism, no longer part of the religion but an identifying sign of the culture. In mourning, everyone pulls together.

It is as though we have the courage to pay the price of war, but lack the courage to pay the price of peace.

Dark thoughts for dark days. Sometimes you question your sanity for being here. In the darkest days of the Yom Kippur War, unable to sleep, I remember picking up an old copy of Theodor Herzl's novel *Altneuland* (Old-New Land), in which he laid out his dream of what Israel could be. It seemed so innocent, so romantic. His dream came true, though not quite in the way he thought. That is the fate of dreams and dreamers.

He took no account of the realities of human failings, and it was that lack of knowledge that allowed him to dream. Too much knowledge burdens you, and naïveté begins to seem enviable. You become nostalgic for it.

Now, as another war was drawing to its close, I came across some lines from a poem of Yehuda Amichai's that mirrored my sadness:

> *I came back once more to this place:*
> *I remember it from the time when hopes*
> *Still looked like the faces that hoped them; . . .*
>
> *But the noble voices that gave*
> *Fateful tidings with quiet words have long been*
> *   silent,*
> *And the echoes are scattered over the whole land*
> *As blessing or curse.*
>
> *And the hopes that once looked like the faces of*
> *those that hoped,*
> *Are now fewer and fewer . . .*

We were on our way to Amichai's house in Yemin Moshe, near where I used to live. As we walked past my house, I held Ya'ir's hand tight at the reminder that it was no longer mine. "Your trouble," he said gently, "is that you're searching for the past, and everything's changed. Israel's changed, Jerusalem's changed. I've changed and so have you. You can't go back to what was. You have to accept what is."

I picked a sprig of rosemary and rubbed it between my thumb and forefinger, the scent of it fresh and damp in the dry air. I let it drop. "No, I have to acknowledge what is, but not necessarily accept it. I know I can't turn the clock backward. For myself and for you, I wouldn't want to. For Israel, I admit I wish I could. But that's not the point: I can't simply accept the changes that have taken place here, because accepting them means a passive assent. And I can't assent to them."

"So what are you going to do? It's hard enough just surviving in this country. You want to fight against the whole way things are going?"

"Yes," I said, feeling oddly defiant. "Oh, yes. I can't conceive of coming back without doing that."

"But you can conceive of coming back?"

I stopped short, realizing what I'd just said. "I don't know if I can come back for good. But I do know I'll keep on coming back." I looked around me — at Yemin Moshe, Mount Zion, Gehenna. "I mean, look. . . . All this is part of me. This, and friends, and lovers." Ya'ir smiled. "There is so much of me here. Leaving for good would be like walking out on myself. And I know it sounds crazy to even think of coming back with everything that's happening, but you see, it hurts just as much to stay away."

Ya'ir hesitated, then gripped my hand hard. "If you do come back," he said, "many people will be very glad . . . and especially me."

XIX

ONCE, Jerusalem's crazies were lovable. At Amichai's, Dennis and Yehuda were reminiscing about them, two poets bent over their wineglasses and affably swapping stories, for all the world as though Yehuda had never written the line "Caution: nostalgic area." That line had been dancing in my mind for weeks.

Dennis missed Kesher Le'Achad — the Link to the One — who used to roam up and down Jaffa Road dressed in outrageously colorful garb for the fifties, with beads piled in profusion around her neck. Nobody ever knew her real name, and it wasn't clear if she remembered it herself. She sold amulets and talismans. And one day, she sold Dennis God's phone number for half a pound.

It was a Jerusalem number, of course. Dennis was curious to find out whose it was, so he called, but there was no answer. He was oddly disappointed. The next time he saw Kesher Le'Achad, he complained: "You know, every time I call that number you sold me, there's nobody there." To which she replied sympathetically: "Well, isn't that just like God, not to answer. . . ."

As we laughed, the drift of the main conversation at the party came through to us. A particularly pompous Princeton academic was talking about how to get the Jews out of Finland.

"Finland?" said Dennis, head on one side, clearly readying for mischief. Yehuda smiled and almost imperceptibly shook his head. Dennis held his peace. We listened desultorily for a few minutes. It seemed that, having solved Israel's problems to his own satisfaction, the Princeton man was now efficiently dealing with those of all the world's Jews.

Yehuda went to make the coffee. He had been very quiet all evening, as he often is. "A very deep man," Princeton confided in me, nodding seriously in the direction of the kitchen. "Very deep."

I felt sorry for him. While he had been pontificating, we had been enjoying ourselves, sifting the stuff of Jerusalem. But then he wasn't interested in that. That was too unreal for him. He was interested only in what he already knew — in making Jerusalem and all who lived in it conform to his own preconceptions. I began to feel some of the resentment I'd been hearing from other Israelis, from public and cultural figures who were all on the informal "must-see" list of visiting journalists and intellectuals. I knew what it felt like, because I too had been on the list.

"I'm tired of all these instant experts," one of the country's leading journalists had said. "They come here for two or three weeks, sometimes only for a few days, and they do the rounds of people you and I know. We trot out our opinions and analyses for them, because somewhere inside us we're still convinced that it matters, and we can't say no, no matter how often we tell ourselves we should. We have this need to keep explaining ourselves. So we become an open book to them — the kind of book you buy at the airport on the way over and then throw away when you catch the plane back."

"We're not real for them," said the head of a major research institute. "They're just using us, practicing being Jewish on us. They see Israelis as projections of themselves, as though we could show them who they are."

And a liberal politician sat back in exhaustion after talking to yet another fact-finding group. "The trouble is that they have a vested interest in an Israel under siege," he said. "They like the old image of a brave little Israel struggling for its survival. They can see that something's changing, but the change itself doesn't really interest them. They only want to know how they should feel about it. They're looking for the correct position to hold at a distance, in New York or Chicago or Los Angeles."

But of course it is a two-way street. This constant flow of important visitors makes the Israelis feel important too. And while Americans search for their Jewishness in the mirror of Israel, the Israelis feel that they're making contact with the world. Yet there is an inevitable distance between Israeli and American Jews. Israel itself looms large between them. Too many American Jews have too much of their identity invested in an idealized, almost mythic Israel. It is essential to their self-respect as Jews, it seems, as though that identity were somehow shabby without it, loose and shapeless like an old coat hopelessly out of style.

"You know, it's as though we here in Israel were the gladiators in a Roman circus," said Ilana one day as we drank coffee in the café just below her office. She savored the idea along with the coffee. "Yes, it's a circus, and Jews abroad are the audience. They adopt us and lay their bets on us, they feed us up and then watch from the stands as we get fed to the lions. They face life and death through us. We do it for them, so that they can remain where they are, safely out of the arena, looking on."

Suddenly she looked embarrassed: "I didn't know I was so bitter about it. But I can't help it. It's true." She took another sip of her coffee, and sat for a moment nursing the cup between her hands. And then very slowly, she raised her head and almost whispered: "But you know, I forgot something: the Christians in the arena survived in history, and the Roman audience disappeared. And I know I shouldn't, but somehow I find that comforting."

Many Israelis are now beginning to grasp that when American Jews fervently defend the symbolic "good Israel," the real place and its people are dehumanized. They don't really exist. And when the real circumstances of your existence are denied by people who profess to have only your best interests at heart, resentment sets in. When the complexities and conflicts and paradoxes of living here are ignored, you feel a deep sense of insult to your own existence.

For Israelis, this country is full of "places where." Where someone died in battle, where someone was injured, where they made love, where they argued, where they heard such and such a thing . . . in short, where they live. The place itself is the raw stuff of the fabric of their lives. But most American Jews have no such associations, and too many still carry another country in their minds — a mixture of Jewish Agency pamphlets and Leon Uris novels, a country that will be what they want, not what exists.

Anyone who has lived in Israel has discovered that you don't have to be religious, speak Yiddish or be obsessed by the Holocaust to be Jewish, Menachem Begin notwithstanding. Neither do you have to support every action of whatever government is in power at the time. Living in Israel does not involve that strange loss of personality that seems to afflict many American Jews whenever Israel is discussed, when they become knee-jerk mouthpieces of a misconceived "pro-Israelism" that has little or nothing to do with Israel's own best interests, and much to do with their own attachment to Israel as a means of being Jewish.

Otherwise liberal American Jews can turn into staunch conservatives as soon as Israel is mentioned. They are cut off from the options, and from the vast range of debate inside Israel. They cannot read the Hebrew papers, let alone the conservative *Yediot Aharonot*'s center page every Friday, which is known with a mixture of affection and irony as "the PLO page" for its left-wing satire and criticism.

Too often, American Jews see anyone who criticizes Israeli government policy as "anti-Israel." Suggest to them that their own criticism of the Nixon or Reagan administration made them anti-American and they would be the first to complain, rightly, of McCarthyism. Yet the standards they hold for their own country apparently do not apply to Israel. If their way of seeing things were to hold sway, then half of all Israelis would have to be called anti-Israel — the absurd result of the peculiar idea that criticism of a democratically elected government means that one is an enemy of that country.

This absurdity stems from the strong desire not to know. Clinging to their symbolic Israel, many American Jews still deny the facts and blame the messengers. Perhaps they should be accounted lucky people after all: they avoid dealing with the messiness of reality. Everything remains clear to them, and the ideal is untarnished.

For a while, in the fifties and sixties, Israel carried the banner for Jewish liberals everywhere. It was Another Country, a foil, a gilded mirror, where the race was to the swift and victory to the just. It was the epitome of Henry V's "we brave few."

But the eighties have badly dented that image. The violent street demonstrations of the Begin years, the stepped-up colonization of the West Bank, the cruel siege of Beirut, the Sabra and Shatila massacres, the Jewish terror network, the Pollard spy case . . . The real problems of Israel became so obvious that there was no longer any way to ignore them — unless, of course, you needed the dream so badly that you were willing to give up your own better judgment in its favor.

I have seen that done. At a lecture in New York by a well-known Israeli rabbi, for example, an American stood to ask a question. A few nights before, he said, three of "our boys" — by which he meant Israeli soldiers — had sat on the floor of his New York apartment telling him of their shame at orders they had followed while doing army service in the West Bank. The orders had included brutality bordering on torture, and they had followed them despite an Israeli law that allows a soldier to refuse to follow an order he believes to be illegal.

"But rabbi," said the questioner, "they cried as they told me about it. And surely, so long as we can still cry, we are not corrupted by what we do?" The rabbi, to my dismay, evaded the question.

It has been said many times, but is no less true for that: occupation degrades the occupier as much as the occupied. As a result, liberals especially feel that Israel has somehow let them down, as though the country were a lover who had chosen somebody else.

To see Israel as human and therefore deeply fallible is the hard position. Far easier, sometimes, to simply resent it for not living up to impossible ideals, and to turn away as did one man after reading an article I had written on Israel's Sephardic majority — the Jews of North African and Middle Eastern origin whose resentment at living in a country devoted to western ideals has led them to the right wing, to a violent anti-Arabism, and sometimes to the state of a mob calling for a "strong leader" and even for a messiah. "Thank God," said this man on finishing the article. "Now I don't have to worry about Israel anymore. It's a foreign country."

I almost envied him the ease with which he could claim foreignness. For a moment, I wanted to be able to do that too, as though I could undo all the years since 1966. A happy fantasy occurred to me: perhaps I too could attain the state of the American Jew. Visit Israel once a year, perhaps, see friends, tour a little, then leave, back to real life elsewhere, in London or New York. But the fantasy dissolved as quickly as it had appeared. I knew I could never do that. Like everything I write about Israel, that article had been written out of a deep love and concern, not out of a disinterested journalistic desire to cover a "good story." I envied that essential detachment that keeps American Jews where they are, in America, yet at the same time the Israeli in me came to the fore with a certain sense of identity: as Israel was now foreign for him, so too was New York for me.

✡

Meanwhile, the flow of visitors to Jerusalem continued unabated. When they are well known, it is fascinating to watch their reactions. We all project ourselves onto foreign places, perhaps in an attempt to make sense of them. And Israel is a palimpsest for visitors. Even the most sophisticated find here what they are ready to find.

A. Alvarez, the literary poker player who goes by the name of Al, arrived from London. "So much doubt here," he said. "So many people with foreheads creased in doubt." Philip Roth flew in from Greece and London and New York, and found "so much passion, everyone so certain." They talked to many of the same people.

Roth, elegant and charming, claimed that he was here just for a vacation — "just to breathe a bit." But writers are not very good at "just breathing." And besides, it was his second visit that year. As though to welcome him, that morning's issue of *Ha'aretz* carried a report on a new immigrant indicted for incitement to violence against Arabs in his Russian-language newspaper. His name was Portnoy.

Modern Israel, veering to extremes, clearly held a fascination for Roth unmatched by the old idealized one. We talked about madmen and psychopaths. He confessed a pull toward them and away from the liberal universalist spokespeople on the usual visitor's list, which he had covered on his first visit. "I come from that kind of world," he said. "I don't need to come to Israel to find liberal humanist Jews. But these extremists, they're fascinating."

True, a novelist could have a ball with a character like Kahane, who had spent years "undercover" with the gentile name of Caine, working as a sports journalist and an FBI informant, and living with a non-Jewish woman who then committed suicide, until he emerged as the great defender with the Jewish Defense League. Such people do indeed exert the fascination of the extreme — of the Jew behaving as Jews are not meant to. They are the unrepentant, guiltless, shameless Jews, the new aggressive and violent Jews, unburdened by conscience. Roth spent hours on the West Bank being lectured by Gush Emunim leaders about "the real Jew," whose values were the polar opposite of the defeatist pacifist "self-hating Jew." That phrase, "self-hating Jew," had become one of the code phrases of the right, used by people so obsessed with self-hate that they grasp at the classic defense of projecting it onto others. It is a powerful threat to many Americans, touching the roots of their own insecurity about their Jewishness. Presented with the choice between being "real" or "self-hating," they give in to demagoguery.

Not Roth; he was too sophisticated for that. He went through successive stages of attraction, amazement, humor and then rejection, and left to write a new novel, another black comedy in the making. "He can call it 'Black Mitzvah,' " Oded joked after Roth's departure. He had liked Roth tremendously, but there was still a touch of resentment there too: "He's toying with us, you know. He doesn't take us seriously. Why should he? We only exist in order to give Zuckerman something interesting to rub up against."

He was right, of course, but then so too, as a writer, was Roth. After all, the vision of a whole nation arguing about whether it is "real" or "self-hating," "normal" or "special," is irresistibly absurd.

XX

"IT'S pathological to have a state and then choose to stay out of it," declared the novelist A. B. Yehoshua one evening. The hall was full of secular Israelis who had come to hear him say just that. They were eagerly groping for a new rationale for their being here.

Yehoshua, otherwise known as Buli, is a short dark man with features so strong that his face seems too small for them. Nose, mouth and eyes are all crowded in with an intensity that matches his style of talking. It is what is known as a very interesting face.

Buli is not religious — if anything, his religion is psychoanalysis — but he does have a mystic concept of Israel. And that leads him into a fervent attack on non-Israeli Jews, or what is known as the Diaspora.

"This is the pathology of the Jews. A unique pathology," he continued. "The Diaspora is a faulty gene. It's a bad chromosome, a cancer." He went on with a virtual torrent of abuse against the Diaspora, and it left me disturbed. There was something in it that almost smacked of antisemitism. It was a modern development of the ideas of the pioneer socialist Zionists earlier in this century, who saw those who stayed in the Diaspora as weaklings and "sheep who went to the slaughter" in the Holocaust. They developed the idea of "the new Jew," who would be as different from the antisemitic stereotype as possible: strong, independent, fearing nobody.

Buli's complaint is that few Jews move to Israel anymore. The number is now down to a few thousand a year, and those are almost entirely religious and right-wing. The old socialist *aliya* is over. Israel no longer attracts liberals, and the various Israeli agencies involved in encouraging *aliya* have practically given up on them. Twice as many Israelis leave every year as come, leading Buli to the exasperated idea that "if there's ever peace with the Arab countries, Israelis will start emigrating to the moon!"

He traced this "pathology" back to the Babylonian exile, in the sixth century B.C. When Jews then could have come back to Israel, most opted to remain where they were, just as do most Jews today. They were afraid to enter their own country, Buli declared, and Zionism only really began when the fear of the Diaspora grew stronger than the fear of Israel.

At this I shifted uncomfortably, remembering an *aliya* activist who had told me that there was now high hope of a massive immigration from South Africa, since Jews there feared the collapse of the white regime. Buli barged onward, building up his argument. Only about 10 percent of those who came to Israel did so of their own free will, he maintained; the rest were refugees of one kind or another. And even then they can't stay. They are afraid. Only in their own land can they lead a full life as Jews, yet they run away from it, back to the Diaspora. And by choosing the Diaspora, he argued, they say no to the task of being special — of being a chosen people. That task can only be fulfilled here, in their own country.

At this point he paused dramatically — this was a well-rehearsed speech, given in kibbutzim and lecture halls throughout the country — and then pronounced: "I think of myself as the total Jew."

Visions of that absurd little book *The Total Woman* came dancing before me in response to all this earnestness. I couldn't see Buli answering the door in black net stockings and a frilly apron, or whatever the Jewish equivalent might be. The idea of "the total Jew" seemed as wonderfully and unintentionally absurd as that of "the total woman," and for a moment I was convulsed in silent laughter.

I didn't laugh long, though. Real Jews, new Jews, total Jews — there is little difference between them, after all. Gush Emunim and Meir Kahane's "boys" also think of themselves as total Jews, and by the same definition. Buli is on the left, they are on the extreme right; yet both are energized by the same idea of chosenness. Both believe in being a special people, redeemed in their own land. And both are spellbound by a vision of pure Jewishness. Gush Emunim and Kahane would achieve this by expelling all Arabs; Buli would achieve it by supporting a Palestinian state, in the hope that Israeli Arabs would then leave Israel and move to the new Palestine (though why he thinks they would behave unlike the Jews remains unclear). The means are different, but the mystical dream is fundamentally the same.

✡

Chosenness. It is surely the bane of nations. Every nation seems to believe itself chosen at one stage or another. Britain was chosen to bring civilization to a primitive world (and to profit very nicely in the process). Iran was chosen to bring the true light of Islam to an unbelieving world. The United States was chosen to protect the free world, and the Soviet Union to bring the benefits of Communism, however dubious, to the third world.

But these global ideas of chosenness are also the downfall of nations. They can unite a nation by giving it a sense of meaning and purpose, true. But they can also make it act in irrational ways, against its own self-interest.

Israel defines itself as a Jewish state. This was its founding purpose. Perhaps, given peace, the idea of being Israeli would have become more important than that of being Jewish. But after nearly forty years of existence, the country is still chronically insecure. And in the last few years, it has looked more to the idea of peoplehood than to nationhood for its sense of identity.

The key idea is now Jewishness rather than Israeliness, and there are solid political reasons for this. In public pronouncements, in street talk, even in songs, the State of Israel is hardly mentioned anymore. Instead, we hear of *Eretz Yisra'el* — the biblical Land of Israel — which is the code phrase for Israel proper plus the West Bank. Few people talk of Israelis anymore, but of *Am Yisra'el* — the People of Israel — meaning Jews only. The new language has filtered down so thoroughly that the phrases have shrunk to single words in speech: *Eretz-rael, Amsrael.* And the theme of the last school year's citizenship program was "One People." Nowhere else in the world, except perhaps in California's Esalen Institute, am I called on to be "one" with everyone around me.

I went to another lecture. You can spend all your time in Jerusalem going to public lectures if you care to, everyone has so much to say. But Yehoshafat Harkabi, formerly head of military intelligence and now a professor of Middle East studies, is unique. He defines himself as "a Machiavellian dove" — a man who is dovish for logical pragmatic reasons, not as an emotional stance. I had liked him ever since studying with him at the Hebrew University in the late sixties.

He was talking about "the heroic stance": the emotional pull of the image promoted by Begin, the image of the world being against us and our need to stand as a persecuted, maligned, misunderstood few against the world. It was a posture, Harkabi said, and during the Begin years, posturing took the place of policy. In Begin's mind, the Lebanon war began as a higher calling. Israel would save the Lebanese Christians, save civilization, redeem itself in the eyes of the Christian world. And this higher calling rode roughshod over Israel's own best interests, blinding the eyes of policymakers to reality, until Sharon could manipulate the whole cabinet just by mouthing the right phrases to Begin, a kind of Rasputin to Begin's Tsar Nicholas, only far more dangerous.

The whole idea of chosenness, Harkabi argued, was mere heroics. The ideology of a chosen people made Israel a tribe in an enemy environment rather than a state in a community of states. The irony of that brought a rueful smile to my face: I had heard something similar from an Egyptian diplomat in Cairo some years before. "Egypt is the only real state in the Middle East," he had said. "All the rest are tribes, with flags."

By now Harkabi was wiping at his forehead and groping to keep to the main thread of his argument. He kept stopping for breath. I had never seen him this emotional. It puzzled me for a while, but as he went on, I thought I recognized the problem. While he could trace the abandonment of reason for mysticism in the start of the Lebanon war with unerring accuracy, he was himself a prisoner of the paradox he attacked. He too was a victim of specialness. He too did not want Israel to be "a normal state." He finally declared as much. "Normality is just a recipe for mediocrity," he said. "I want this country to be better."

I recognized it, all right. We all struggle with this inherent contradiction. Only the extreme right is exempt from it. We want to be like any other country, yet that is the thing we most fear. We would lose our specialness. We yearn for normality, but are also terrified of it. We are still in thrall to Ben-

Gurion's idea of Israel as "a light unto the nations." And though in Ben-Gurion's lifetime he so hated Begin that he would refer to him only as "that man," the two were not so far apart as it may seem. They shared the basic idea of Israel as a means of redemption for the Jews.

It is of course a religious idea, but it was central to the vision of the socialist Zionist pioneers, who were resolutely secular. They came here "to build a country and be rebuilt by it" — to be born anew, as Ben-Gurion said he was on the day he arrived here from eastern Europe. But you can secularize a religious idea only at great risk. If those founding Zionists could really turn in their graves, this whole country would be in constant earthquake from all the turning being done. Perhaps inevitably, the secular metaphor has returned to its origin in religion.

✡

"Why do the Jews have to have a purpose? Why can't we just be?" I asked Yossi Klein, a gentle, soft-spoken man who thinks of himself as "a new-age messianist." Hard to imagine when you talk with him that he used to be one of Kahane's adherents in the Jewish Defense League in the States.

"Because that's what's meant to be," he answered, smiling.

I tried Avi Ravitzky, a lecturer in Jewish philosophy and one of the founders of Oz Ve'Shalom and Netivot Shalom ("Courage and Peace" and "Ways of Peace"), which together form a kind of religious Peace Now movement. "Why do we have to redeem ourselves all the time?" I asked. "Why do we have to be so restless? Why can't we just allow ourselves a bit of peace?"

He also smiled. "Just a bit of rest would do," he replied. "But the fact is that with so much that's happened here, there's no way anyone connected with the religious sources can ignore the issue of redemption or messianism. They are forced to take a stand on it, since it's clear that the normalization of the Jewish people hasn't worked. That should come as no surprise, since as you say, secular Zionism was also messianic, based on the idea of redemption."

But secular Zionism was never a false Judaism, I argued. And therein lay a difference that packed a vengeance. The messianism of Gush Emunim was violent and immoral; they saw redemption as coming out of the barrel of a gun.

Avi nodded sadly. "It's easy to be moral when you don't have a gun. We could keep high standards throughout history because we were powerless. Now thank God we do have power, and now is the real test of morality. And if we expel and mistreat and kill others in the street, then we annul not only the present but the whole Jewish past too. So in that sense I'm fighting for the Jewish past as well as for the future."

He knows that the religious doves have little chance of influencing matters in the short run, but he hopes their time will come. "If there is even a partial withdrawal from the West Bank, there'll be a huge theological crisis, because right-wing religious circles will see it as taking a step backward from the days of the messiah. And then I hope that we can fill the vacuum, providing a third option between religious hawkishness and secular dovishness. We can do that because ours is a nondeterministic approach to messianism, where Gush Emunim's is deterministic. We don't see the State of Israel as the means to redemption, but as an option for it."

So much talk of redemption was exhausting. Questions swirled through my mind without answers. What was it to be a "normal state" in any case? Or a special one? The whole issue seemed absurd, as though we could determine such things, let alone control them. Yet here I had been puzzling at it for days, as deeply bound as anyone else into this paradox of being both special and normal at the same time.

Clearly, that is impossible, unless it is normal to be special. In fact, that may well be. The idea of specialness is always tempting, and we all like to think of ourselves as special in some way.

At this point, my mind began to turn in circles, swooping down like the blackest of hawks to a strange kind of fatalism. Perhaps it was easier for this country to be special than normal. After all, peace is hard work. Boring work, even. It wouldn't make the headlines of the world's papers every day. And perhaps that would frighten us, make us doubtful somehow of the reality of our own existence.

This is not a restful country, there is no doubt of that. And not a restful people, either. Maybe normality is simply impossible for such a country and such a people. Maybe after so many centuries of wandering and of being the outsiders, we simply cannot tolerate the idea of it.

Yet something is changing, and light breaks into that dark circle of thinking. Being special is exhausting, and especially after the Lebanon war, more and more Israelis are feeling that exhaustion.

The whole idea of Zionism was to make a special state — a Jewish state — where any Jew, from anywhere in the world, would be guaranteed automatic citizenship under the Law of Return. This law has been the cornerstone of Zionism, of the whole idea of "the in-gathering of the exiles." It makes every Jew in the world a potential Israeli. But many Israelis now suspect that the days of Zionism are over. Nearly 40 percent of Israelis in their thirties do not even see themselves as Zionists. They feel no need for Zionism. They are Israelis, born here in their own country, and they want to live in their own country as other people do in theirs — in peace and quiet.

This is the generation of the Yom Kippur War, the first losing war that Israel fought. It was a technical victory, to be sure, but it was experienced as a defeat, and seemed to mark a turnaround in Israel's military fortunes. That war broke many myths. No special star guided the Israel Defense Forces in 1973, as it seemed to in 1967. Instead, there was a normal tale of human error, and a high price to pay for it. The generation now in its thirties paid the bulk of that price. And perhaps as a result, it silently agrees with Meron Benvenisti when he advocates repealing the Law of Return.

"As long as this law exists," he says, "the idea of redemption will continue — the idea that this state exists for something other than itself. My ideal is that on the fiftieth Independence Day, in 1998, we'll be able to annul that law — we'll be able to say that from now on, this country belongs to those who live in it." A country to live in, not to redeem oneself and others in. A normal country.

Once the withdrawal from Lebanon began, that idea began to seem possible. The heroics of the Begin era seemed to be over, at least on the level of government, and the accession of Shimon Peres as prime minister brought a new tone of reason and moderation, a vast relief after the hysterics of the Begin years. But Peres came to power in a country that was deeply split politically, his hands tied by a national unity government. And the spirit of Begin still hovered over the country as extremists raised the tone of violence and racism.

Begin himself remained silent, closed up in his Jerusalem apartment and refusing interviews. Rumors circulated about whether he was even still alive. "Free Menachem Begin!" read a piece of graffiti scrawled on a wall near the center of town.

"He must realize what he's done, surely," I said to Oded at the Tsrif. "Lebanon, Kahane, the economic mess — he knows what he's done to this country, and that's why he's sunk into this depression. But you know, he always was an honest man, however much I disagreed with his policies. And he still has huge public status, so that one strong statement from him could do a lot to stop a Kahane in his tracks. If I were Begin, I think I'd want to speak out once more before I died — to address the nation, say I was wrong, and apologize. He might still do that, you know. I think he just might."

Oded shook his head sorrowfully like a teacher disappointed in a star pupil. "The trouble with you," he said, "is that you're a romantic."

But then so were we all, once.

XXI

My last Shabbat, and breakfast at Dan's, with bacon popping in the pan and prayer rumbling from the synagogue nearby.

We talked as though I wasn't going anywhere; we had never been very good at goodbyes, and time hadn't improved our abilities. Instead, I tried out on him a new kind of optimism that had been building in me over the past week or so — a shift in point of view, as it were.

We could be entering a stage where rational decisions took the place of emotional posturing, I reasoned. Instead of Begin, we now had the calmer, more mature approach of Shimon Peres. In fact, perhaps those seven years of Beginism had been a necessary stage in Israel's development, a kind of adolescent acting-out. And now that we had worn ourselves to exhaustion with all that high drama, we were ready to come to adulthood as a nation.

Dan looked at me quizzically across the table, orange juice untouched in front of him. "Go on," he said.

"This may be terrible to say, but we might have needed Lebanon to show us once and for all that military solutions won't work. That in the adult world, there are no quick solutions. That we have to learn to compromise, to accept reality and find ways to live with it without being self-destructive. It could even be that the Lebanon war was a bad overdose of the excitement we're so addicted to here, and that now we're sobering up and beginning to recover from it.''

Dan downed the orange juice and considered the idea for a moment over his empty glass. ''There's such a thing as permanent brain damage from an overdose,'' he said. ''You see what's going on with Kahane. Are you sure you're not over-reaching for hope?''

The question caught me off balance, breaking the stride of my hard-won optimism. ''I don't know . . .'' I looked at him bleakly, the flow of words stopped short. Of course I was reaching for hope. Without hope there is no future. And it could very well be that my need for hope made me reach too far. But I couldn't acknowledge that, not out loud.

Neither of us could foresee the next few months. Just when it seemed that Israelis might indeed have been worn down by war-weariness into considering some form of accommodation with the Palestinians, Palestinian terrorism began to increase. It was as though there were some balance of energy at work, and as it fell on one side, it rose on the other. Israelis began to panic as Jews in the West Bank were shot and stabbed whenever opportunity presented itself. These attacks fed the cause of Israeli ultranationalists, who raised the cry for revenge and harsh repression. The extremists on both sides fulfilled each others' expectations; they had a common language of hate, making a Kahane far closer to a Palestinian terrorist than to most of the Israeli public. In fact, they could have been working together toward the same end: perpetuating the cycle of violence and frustrating any move toward peace. That was the real brain damage, on both sides. And the question was whether the rest of us, also on both sides, had the strength to fight it.

✡

I was going over to Ilana and David's the next afternoon, but first I took a long solitary walk down into Gehenna, needing to say goodbye to places as well as to people. Donkeys brayed from one hillside, goats from another, as the afternoon sun gentled the harsh landscape. That old sense of innocence came back to me but it came at a distance now. Experience had changed me, as it had changed this place. I looked back fondly at the girl who had come here twenty years before, knowing that I could neither retrieve the past nor escape it. The past is what makes us who we are today.

By the time I turned to leave, I was feeling quite mellow. I took the steep path leading up out of the valley. An Arab construction worker was on his way down, probably going home from his job on a building site in West Jerusalem. He was in his fifties, and his face, hands, clothes and keffiya were full of dust from the day's work.

We passed each other, and he was about ten yards below me when there was a sharp pain at the back of my ankle. A small stone went skittering off it to the side of the path. I turned and looked down at the ankle — just a scrape — and then on down the path. The man was just standing there, staring at me, as though waiting for something.

I bent down and picked up the stone. "Did you throw this?" I asked. It was an unnecessary question; there was nobody else around.

He said nothing — just bent down and picked up another stone.

There was no thought in my head other than absolute anger that anyone should throw a stone at me. Nobody had thrown a stone at me before, ever. Aiming deliberately wide, I threw the stone back. It hit a tree trunk to his left, then clattered down onto the path. His arm came up to throw the new stone he had in his hand.

"Don't throw that at me," I said. "Nobody throws stones at me."

He hesitated, arm still raised. I stood there, facing him down, angry at the stupidity of this scene, angry at him for forcing me into it, angry at myself for having thrown a stone at an Arab.

He lowered his arm. I had to put an end to this. I turned, and with what I hoped was slow determination, went on up the path, wondering if I was not about to get a shower of stones in my back. I didn't. At the top, I looked back. He was still there, unmoving, just staring. Anger, resentment, hate — a whole mix of emotions seemed to flow up the stretch of path between us. Suddenly I felt sick at myself. At the moment I had thrown that stone back, I had felt very Israeli.

I was still disturbed by the confrontation when I got to Ilana's. She grimaced when I told her about it. She shrugged, she sighed, she did all the things that one can do. "What made you think you were impervious to it all?" she said finally. "It affects all of us, sooner or later. What else could you have done? It was a no-win situation, no matter what. Who knows why he threw that stone? He may have had a hard day at work, or he may have been trying to get your attention, or he may have just seen an Israeli walking alone and taken the opportunity to cast his own stone. But it doesn't even matter, really. The fact is that the minute the stone is thrown, he becomes an Arab, you a Jew. That's the way it is here now. It will never be like New Zealand, you know. Not here."

I smiled sadly. That was undeniably true. Yet as we sat drinking mint tea under the tall pines of Ilana's garden, a certain calm began to return to me. Crumbs dropped around us as a crow in one of the higher branches ate a piece of stale bread it had found, and a turtledove strutted on the grass nearby, picking up the droppings. I blinked up into the sun, wondering why Jerusalem couldn't always be like this — sun, pines, a good friend, a peaceful end to an afternoon. There were other, smaller New Zealands, I thought, places in our lives where we could find peace with friends and lovers, even in the midst of violence and unrest. There were the fresh green places of the mind that we nurtured in the image of what might someday be possible. And there could be solitary moments of peace too, the more treasured because so hard to find here, like hidden mounds of moss beneath the trees on the north side of a stony hill. And whenever we found them, as I had that afternoon walking in Gehenna, there would always be someone to throw the stone, to break the spell and bring us back to the harshness of reality.

✡

Reality defies neat endings. I had come back to make a separate, personal peace with this place, hoping to write the final chapter in the story of myself and Jerusalem. But my final chapter wasn't going the way I'd planned. The Jewish boy had yelled *"Ruh min hon,"* "Get out of here." The Arab man had thrown stones. Yet instead of saying *Adieu,* I was saying *Au revoir.* And I was saying it in full awareness of what I could come back to.

This fact had made me a source of considerable puzzlement to many people. "But why?" a reporter interviewing me for the local paper had asked. "You're a liberal, you're a dove, and since you write in English you can make your living anywhere in the world. Why break head and heart here?"

We'd talked for two hours, yet still couldn't find an answer to satisfy him. "Look, I tried," I said. "I did everything I could to leave. So maybe it's just not possible. Maybe this place is just not leavable. You can fool yourself that you've left, as I did, but there's something that keeps bringing you back. It's sun and stone and thorns, perhaps. It's the hills of Jerusalem. It's people — a depth of friendship I don't know anywhere else in the world. And it's more than all those together."

I had shrugged. So had he. Perhaps he realized that there could be no satisfying answer.

That last afternoon in Ilana's garden, as she refilled the glasses of mint tea, I told her about the reporter and his question. She nodded in sympathy with my confusion. "It could be that the real question is not whether you'll come back, but whether you ever really left. This place made you who you are. If you turn your back on it, you turn your back on yourself."

I must have been smiling that rueful smile again, because Ilana looked at me and then kept right on talking. "Look," she said, "the fact is that there's a link between place and person, and you haven't found it anywhere else as strongly as you find it here. So you won't come back here for ideology, or because things are as you would want them to be. You won't come back because it's good here. It isn't. You'll come back because despite everything, it's still the place where you feel at home."

Perhaps she was right. All I knew for sure was that I had tried to force a decision, and found out that it couldn't be done. I had discovered what I knew all along but had refused to acknowledge: for anyone who has ever lived here, Israel is never over, no matter what happens. The worse it becomes, the more it hurts, that's all. There is no escaping the involvement. The bond is too deep.

I had wanted to rest from Israel, but I couldn't. It wouldn't let me go, and it wouldn't let me make my peace. "My vampire land," one poet calls it. A land that devours its inhabitants. A land that offers brief moments of tranquillity and then harshly undoes them. A land that frustrates those in search of peace, if it does not kill them. A land where you want so much that you hardly know anymore how to define it. A land that binds you. A land that never lets you rest.